Level 1 · Book 2

Themes

Home, Sweet Home

I Am Brave

CALIFORNIA

SRA Imagine It!

Level 1
Book 2

Program Authors

Carl Bereiter

Andy Biemiller

Joe Campione

Doug Fuchs

Lynn Fuchs

Steve Graham

Karen Harris

Karen Hayashi

Jan Hirshberg

Anne McKeough

Peter Pannell

Michael Pressley

Marsha Roit

Marlene Scardamalia

Marcy Stein

Gerald H. Treadway Jr.

McGraw Hill SRA

Columbus, OH

Acknowledgments

Grateful acknowledgment is given to the following publishers and copyright owners for permissions granted to reprint selections from their publications. All possible care has been taken to trace ownership and secure permission for each selection included. In case of any errors or omissions, the Publisher will be pleased to make suitable acknowledgments in future editions.

Home, Sweet Home

HOMES by Abby Jackson © 2004 by Capstone Press. All rights reserved.
BUILDING A HOUSE COPYRIGHT © 1981 BY BYRON BARTON. Illustrations copyright © 1981 by BYRON BARTON. Used by permission of HarperCollins Publishers.
From: THE WHITE HOUSE by Lloyd G. Douglas. Copyright © 2003 by Rosen Book Works, Inc.
From ALWAYS WONDERING by Aileen Fisher. Copyright © 1991 Aileen Fisher. Used by permission of Marian Reiner on behalf of the Boulder Public Library Foundation, Inc.
PATTERNS OF LIFE: FINDING SHELTER by Daphne Butler. Reproduced by permission of Hodder and Stoughton Limited.
"Home" from THE BIG BOOK OF CLASSROOM POEMS by Kathleen M. Hollenbeck. Published by Teaching Resources/Scholastic Inc. Copyright © 2004 by Kathleen M. Hollenbeck. Reproduced by permission.
THIS HOUSE IS MADE OF MUD. Text copyright © 1991 by Ken Buchanan. Illustrations copyright © 1991 by Libba Tracy. Reprinted by permission of Northland Publishing, LLC.

I Am Brave

MY BROTHER IS AFRAID OF JUST ABOUT EVERYTHING by Lois Osborn. Copyright (c) 1982. Reprinted by permission of Browne & Miller Literary Associates, Chicago, IL.
THERE'S A BIG, BEAUTIFUL WORLD OUT THERE! By Nancy Carlson. Copyright © 2002 Nancy Carlson. All rights reserved including the right of reproduction in whole or in part in any form. This edition published by arrangement with Viking Children's Books, a member of Penguin Young Readers Group, a division of Penguin Group (USA) Inc.
"Night Comes" From A BUNCH OF POEMS AND VERSES by Beatrice Schenk de Regniers. Copyright © 1977 by Beatrice Schenk de Regniers. Used by permission of Marian Reiner. Illustration by Emma Shaw-Smith. Used by permission of Barefoot Books.
CLYDE MONSTER by Robert Crowe and illustrated by Kay Chorao. Text copyright © 1976 by Robert Crowe, 1976. Illustrations copyright © Kay Chorao, 1976. All rights reserved including the right of reproduction in whole or in part in any form. This edition published by arrangement with Dutton Children's Books, a member of Penguin Young Readers Group, a division of Penguin Group (USA) Inc.
IRA SLEEPS OVER by Bernard Waber. Copyright © 1972 by Bernard Waber. Reprinted by permission of Houghton Mifflin Company. All rights reserved.

Photo Credits

vi (tr) © Peter Beck/CORBIS; vi (cl) © Wolfgang Kaehler/CORBIS; vii (tr) © Dennis O'Clair/Getty Images, Inc.; vii (cr) © Stephen Dalton/NHPA Ltd.; 10–11 © Gavin Hellier/Getty Images, Inc.; 14–15 © Lester Lefkowitz/CORBIS; 16 © Dick Luria/Getty Images, Inc.; 17 © Ariel Skelley/CORBIS; 18 © Peter Beck/CORBIS; 19 © PhotoDisc/Getty Images, Inc.; 20 © Caroline von Tuempling/Getty Images, Inc.; 21 © Johner/Getty Images, Inc.; 22 © Peter Turnley/CORBIS; 23 © Steve Vidler/SuperStock; 25 © Grayce Roessler/Index Stock Imagery, Inc.; 26 © Bruno Morandi/Getty Images, Inc.; 24 © Lester Lefkowitz/CORBIS; 27 © Kevin Fleming/CORBIS; 28 © Scott Christopher/Index Stock Imagery, Inc.; 29 © Blend Images/Getty Images, Inc.; 30 (inset) © Lester Lefkowitz/CORBIS, (bkgd) © Grayce Roessler/Index Stock Imagery, Inc.; 31 © Peter Beck/CORBIS; 32–33 © Digital Vision/Getty Images, Inc.; 33 (l) © Mark Chappell/Animals Animals/Earth Scenes, (r) © Kennan Ward/CORBIS; 36–37 © Diana Frances Jones; Gallo Images/CORBIS; 38 (t) © Wayne Walton/Getty Images, Inc., (bl) © Nicholas DeVore/Tony Stone Images, (br) © Blair Seitz/Photo Researchers, Inc.; 39 (tl) © Wolfgang Kaehler/Corbis, (br) © Focus/Moller/Woodfin Camp & Associates; 40 (tl) © Craig Aurness/CORBIS, (tr) © Peter Adams/Getty Images, Inc., (br) © Dietrich Rose/zefa/CORBIS; 41 (t) © Digital Vision/Getty Images, Inc., (br) © Momatiuk/Eastcott/Woodfin Camp & Associates; 42 (t) © José Fuste Rage/zefa/CORBIS, (b) © Karen Beattie/Alamy; 43 (t) © Craig Aurness/Woodfin Camp & Associates, (br) © David Hiser/Tony Stone Images; 44 (t) © Hilarie Kavanagh/Tony Stone Images, (b) © Macduff Everton/CORBIS; 45 (l) Paul Chesley/National Geographic Society Image Collection, (r) ©Tony Arruza/CORBIS; 46 (t) © Wolfgang Kaehler/CORBIS, (b) © Kevin Fleming/CORBIS; 47 (t) © Chad Ehlers/Alamy, (b) ©Sylvain Grandadam/Getty Images, Inc.; 48 (t) E G Company; 48–49 (bkgd) © Wayne Walton/Getty Images, Inc.; 58 courtesy of Bound to Stay Books, Inc.; 64–65 (bkgd) © Dennis O'Clair/Getty Images, Inc.; 66 © Royalty-Free/CORBIS; 67 © Brooks Kraft/CORBIS; 68 (t) © Alan Schein Photography/CORBIS, © PhotoDisc/Getty Images, Inc.; 69 © Stanley Tretick/Sygma/CORBIS; 70, 71 © Bettmann/CORBIS; 72 White House Historical Association; 73 © Wally McNamee/CORBIS; 74 © Lake County Museum/CORBIS; 75 © AFP/Getty Images, Inc.; 76 © Stock Connection Distribution/Alamy; 77 © Lester Lefkowitz/CORBIS; 78–79 © PhotoDisc/Getty Images, Inc.; 86 © Creatas/PunchStock; 87 © PhotoDisc/Getty Images, Inc.; 88–89 © Stephen Dalton/NHPA Ltd.; 90 © Adrienne Gibson/Animals Animals/Earth Scenes; 91 © Michael S. Bisceglie/Animals Animals/Earth Scenes; 92 © Kit Houghton/CORBIS; 93 © Frank Lukasseck/zefa/CORBIS; 94 © Stephen Dalton/NHPA Ltd.; 95 © Paul Nicklen/National Geographic Society, Image Collection; 96 © Martin Harvey/NHPA Ltd.; 97 © Paul A. Souders/CORBIS; 98 © Zigmund Leszczynski/Animals Animals/Earth Scenes; 99 (tl) © Roger Tidman/NHPA/Photoshot, (tr, b) © W. Perry Conway/CORBIS; 100 © Ute & Juergen Schimmelpfenning/zefa/CORBIS; 101 © George Bernard/Animals Animals/Earth Scenes; 102 (cr) © Jeff Bergdoll/Animal Animals/Earth Scenes, (bl) © Hal Beral/CORBIS; 103 (tr) © Anthony Bannister/NHPA Ltd., (cl) © Dietrich Rose/zefa/CORBIS; 104 © Lance Nelson/Stock Photos/zefa/CORBIS; 105 © Felix St Clair Renard/Getty Images, Inc.; 106 (cl) © W. Perry Conway/CORBIS, (bc) © Felix St Clair Renard/Getty Images, Inc., (br) © Hal Beral/CORBIS; 136 (t) courtesy of Ken Buchanan, (b) courtesy of Libbra Tracy; 172 (t) Lois Osborn; 172 (b) courtesy of Erica Villnave; 174–175 © Digital Vision/Getty Images, Inc.; 175 © Michael Newman/PhotoEdit; 198 courtesy of Nancy Carlson; 222 (t) © Merle Fox Photography; 222 (b) Kay Chorao; 230 (t) © Scala/Art Resource, NY, (b) courtesy of Gene Barretta; 266 courtesy of Bernard Waber; 268–269 © OSF/Stan Osolinski/Animals Animals/Earth Scenes; 269 © Robert Brenner/PhotoEdit.

English-Language Arts Content Standards for California Public Schools reproduced by permission, California Department of Education, CDE Press, 1430 N Street, Suite 3207, Sacramento, CA 95814.

SRAonline.com

 SRA

Send all inquiries to this address:
SRA/McGraw-Hill
4400 Easton Commons
Columbus, OH 43219-6188

ISBN: 978-0-07-621375-7
MHID: 0-07-621375-7

1 2 3 4 5 6 7 8 9 RRW 13 12 11 10 09 08

The McGraw·Hill Companies

Program Authors

Carl Bereiter, Ph.D.
University of Toronto

Andy Biemiller, Ph.D.
University of Toronto

Joe Campione, Ph.D.
University of California, Berkeley

Doug Fuchs, Ph.D.
Vanderbilt University

Lynn Fuchs, Ph.D.
Vanderbilt University

Steve Graham, Ed.D.
Vanderbilt University

Karen Harris, Ed.D.
Vanderbilt University

Karen Hayashi
Former Administrator, Elk Grove
Unified School District,
Elk Grove, California

Jan Hirshberg, Ed.D.
Reading Specialist

Anne McKeough, Ph.D.
University of Toronto

Peter Pannell
Principal, Eliot Middle School,
Altadena, California

Michael Pressley, Ph.D.
Michigan State University

Marsha Roit, Ed.D.
National Reading Consultant

Marlene Scardamalia, Ph.D.
University of Toronto

Marcy Stein, Ph.D.
University of Washington, Tacoma

Gerald H. Treadway, Jr., Ed.D.
San Diego State University

Unit 9 Table of Contents

Home, Sweet Home

Home, Sweet Home

Throughout the world, animals and people make homes from materials they find. Are all homes alike? What makes a good home for all the different people and animals in the world?

Theme Connection

Look at the photo of colorful houses on Chiappini Street, Bo Kaap, Muslim-Cape Malay area, Cape Town, South Africa, Africa. What is different about the homes in this photo?

BIG
Idea

Why are homes
important?

11

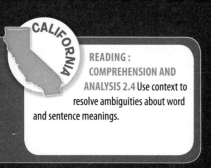

CALIFORNIA

READING : COMPREHENSION AND ANALYSIS 2.4 Use context to resolve ambiguities about word and sentence meanings.

Read the article to find the meanings of:

✦ packed
✦ clay
✦ simple
✦ at hand
✦ shelter
✦ roof
✦ home
✦ sturdy

Vocabulary Development

Context Clues are hints in the text. They help you find the meanings of words. Look at the word *packed*. Use context clues to find the word's meaning.

Vocabulary

Warm-Up

Steve had a packed suitcase—it was very full. In the middle, he placed the clay dog he made in art class. "I hope it will not be smashed by these clothes," Steve said.

"I think it will be safe," said his mother. "The clothes are a simple way to keep it safe. The woven napkins you made are at hand too," she said. She handed Steve the napkins. "You can use them to keep the clay from sticking to your clothes."

Moving Truck

Steve was happy his family was moving. His house was always too cold or too hot. It wasn't a very good shelter anymore. Steve's new house had a new roof. It would help keep the house warm.

"Our new home will be as sturdy as a rock!" Steve joked.

"It will be the best house we've ever had!" said his father.

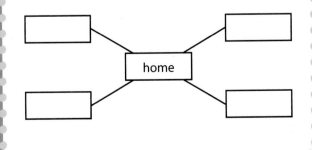

CALIFORNIA

HISTORY-SOCIAL SCIENCE 1.2.4 Describe how location, weather, and physical environment affect the way people live, including the effects on their food, clothing, shelter, transportation, and recreation.

Genre

Informational Writing informs or explains something real.

Comprehension Strategy

★ **Asking Questions**

As you read, ask yourself questions to help you better understand the selection.

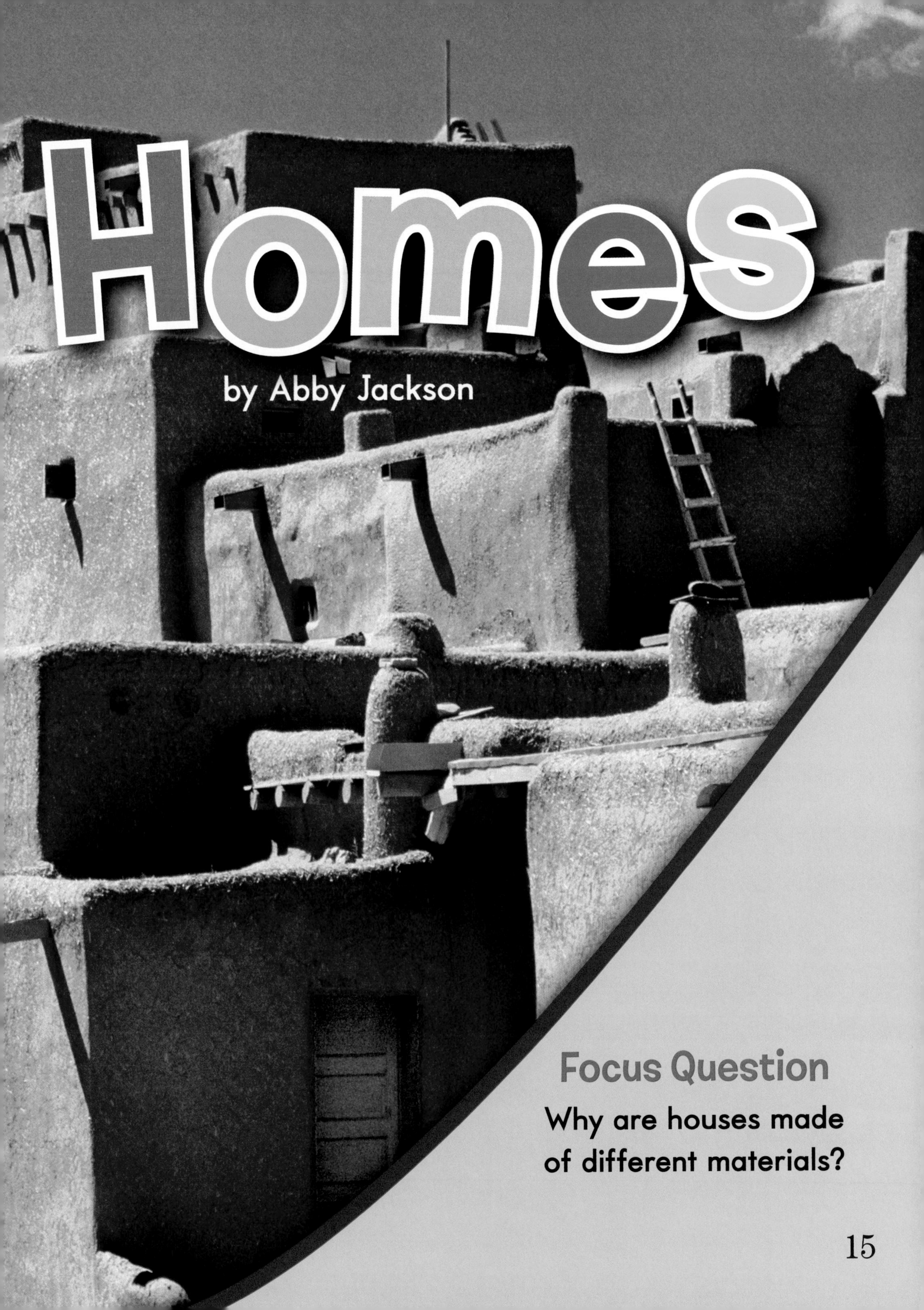

Homes

by Abby Jackson

Focus Question

Why are houses made
of different materials?

What Is a Home?

What is a home? A home is the place where we live. It is a place where we feel safe.

It is a place to return to at the end of the day. A home is a place to cook, eat, and sleep.

A home gives us shelter. Its walls keep in heat. Its roof keeps out rain and snow.

All of these things make a home.
But homes do not look the same
everywhere.

Using What Is at Hand

There are many kinds of homes.
People make their homes from what
is at hand.

This home is made of wood. Wood is easy to build with.

This home is made of sticks
and packed mud. Mud makes a
sturdy house.

This home has a roof made of grass. The grass is woven tightly to keep out rain.

This home is in the desert. It is made
of baked clay. The clay keeps the
house cool.

This home is in the Arctic. It is made from blocks of ice and snow. Yet people stay warm inside.

Homes on the Move

Some people are always moving from place to place. They build simple homes wherever they go.

They can build their homes quickly.
These homes are simple but sturdy.

Some of these homes are made of sticks and branches. Others are made of blankets.

These homes keep people safe from wind and sand. They are also easy to pick up and move.

Your Home

People live in different kinds of homes. What is your home like?

Meet the Author

Abby Jackson

Abby Jackson is a pseudonym, or made-up name, for the author of "Homes." Some authors use made-up names to hide their identities.

WRITING: ORGANIZATION AND FOCUS 1.2 Use descriptive words when writing. **HISTORY-SOCIAL SCIENCE 1.2.4** Describe how location, weather, and physical environment affect the way people live, including the effects on their food, clothing, shelter, transportation, and recreation.

Theme Connections

Discuss

Within the Selection

1. Where do you live if your house is made of ice and snow?

2. Where do you live if your house is made of clay?

3. Why are homes made of different materials?

Beyond the Selection

4. How would you decorate your home?

Write

Describe what kind of home you would like to have when you grow up.

Read

To learn more about homes, look for books or magazine articles about homes to read on your own.

CALIFORNIA

READING: STRUCTURAL FEATURES OF INFORMATIONAL MATERIALS 2.1 Identify text that uses sequence or other logical order. LIFE SCIENCE 2.a Know different plants and animals inhabit different kinds of environments and have external features that help them thrive in different kinds of places.

Genre

Expository Text contains facts about real people and events.

Text Feature

Headings tell you what a paragraph will be about.

Science Link

Strong Homes

Warm Homes

People who live in cold areas need homes to stay warm. Some people use igloos for shelter.

Sturdy Homes

People make their homes sturdy. They build them to keep out rain, snow, ice, and heat. Wood, bricks, and stones make strong homes.

Animal Homes

Animals need good homes too. The kangaroo rat is a desert animal. It lives in a burrow under the ground. The burrow is a shelter that keeps desert animals cool during the day.

Polar bears are arctic animals. They make snowy dens for shelter.

1. How are the headings helpful?

2. How are animal and people homes alike? How are they different?

3. How are kangaroo rat and polar bear homes similar? How are they different?

CALIFORNIA WebLink

Visit **ImagineItReading.com /AtHome** for more information about animal and people homes.

Apply

As you continue your investigations, list any questions you have about homes.

CALIFORNIA

READING:
COMPREHENSION AND
ANALYSIS 2.4 Use context to
resolve ambiguities about word
and sentence meanings.

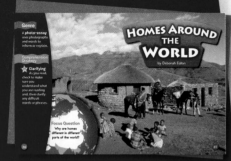

Read the article to find the meanings of:

✦ porch
✦ bulldozer
✦ cement
✦ electrician
✦ hut
✦ builders
✦ bricklayers
✦ chimney

Vocabulary Development

Context Clues are hints in the text. They help you find the meanings of words. Look at the words *bulldozer, bricklayers,* and *porch.* Use context clues to find each word's meaning.

Vocabulary

Warm-Up

Gabe saw a bulldozer moving dirt. "What are they doing?" asked Gabe.

"The builders are making our house," said Gabe's dad. "First the builders dig a hole for the basement. Then they'll pour cement for the floor. The cement will dry. Then they'll build the rest of the house. Each worker has a job. The bricklayers make

walls with bricks. The electrician puts in the wires for lights," said Gabe's dad. Gabe's dad had papers. "These papers show how the workers will make our house. Our house will have a porch so we can sit outside. We'll be protected from sun and rain. The house will also have a chimney. We can have fires in the winter. The chimney will take the smoke away from the house. We could build a hut, or fort, with the materials that are left."

Gabe drew on his own paper. "I'm drawing what I want my hut to look like!" Gabe said.

Vocabulary Word Play

Respond to the following statements with the thumbs-up or thumbs-down sign.

An *electrician* pours *cement* for the floors of new houses.

A *porch* is inside a house.

A *bulldozer* is used to dig holes and move dirt.

Concept Vocabulary

The concept word for this lesson is ***process.*** A process is a series of actions. These actions help you get what you want. Why is building a house such a long process? Why is painting at the end of the process?

Genre

A **photo-essay** uses photographs and words to inform or explain.

Comprehension Strategy

☆ **Clarifying**
As you read, check to make sure you understand what you are reading, and then clarify any difficult words or phrases.

Focus Question

Why are homes different in different parts of the world?

HOMES AROUND THE WORLD

by Deborah Eaton

Here you will see many homes
and many faces in many different
far-off places.

Argentina

Lesotho, South Africa

The Philippines

Mali

Cliff houses are cool
when the sun is hot.

Germany

It's not too hot here. Grass grows
on a roof.

A reed hut is made of dried plants.

Peru

You need a ladder to get to some pueblo houses.

New Mexico, USA

Austria

Flowers make this home pretty.

Their house is up on stilts.

The Philippines

Poland

His house has a tin roof.

Trailers are homes on wheels.

Utah, USA

Kerala, India

Some homes float.

Some homes fold right up.

Morocco

People can even turn
palm leaves into a home.

Guatemala

A porch is a nice place to sit.

Thailand

A fireplace warms a home.

Taos Pueblo, New Mexico, USA

44

China

Doors are for friends coming in.

Windows let light in and let people smile out.

West Indies

Big and tall . . .

Indonesia

Somalia

round and small . . .

all over the world, homes are
for living . . .

Zimbabwe

Utah, USA

and homes are for enjoying.

Meet the Author

Deborah Eaton

Deborah Eaton decided to become a writer when she was sixteen years old. She has written many other books. She lives in Maine and has a cat named Pudge that sits in the window and waves at people as they pass the house. Eaton says she loves all kinds of animals, except for the squirrels that live in her attic!

CALIFORNIA

READING: COMPREHENSION AND ANALYSIS 2.7 Retell the central ideas of simple expository or narrative passages. NARRATIVE ANALYSIS 3.3 Recollect, talk, and write about books read during the school year. WRITING: ORGANIZATION AND FOCUS 1.2 Use descriptive words when writing.

Theme Connections

Discuss

Within the Selection

1. How are plants used in building homes?

2. What kind of home can float?

Across Selections

3. How are the homes in "Homes Around the World" similar to the homes in "Homes"?

Beyond the Selection

4. What could you do to make a house look pretty outside?

Write

Describe the kinds of materials you could use to build a house.

Read

To learn more about homes, look for books or magazine articles about homes to read on your own.

CALIFORNIA

READING:
COMPREHENSION AND
ANALYSIS 2.2 Respond to
who, what, when, where, and
how questions. HISTORY-SOCIAL SCIENCE
1.6.2 Identify the specialized work that
people do to manufacture, transport, and
market goods and services and the
contributions of those who work in
the home.

Genre

Informational Writing informs or explains something real.

Comprehension Skill

☆ **Classify and Categorize**
As you read, group together things and ideas that are alike.

Building a HOUSE

written and illustrated by Byron Barton

Focus Questions

What kinds of workers help build a house? What things do people use to build a house?

On a green hill a bulldozer
digs a big hole.

Builders hammer and saw.

A cement mixer pours cement.

Bricklayers lay large white blocks.

Carpenters come and make a wooden floor.

They put up walls.

They build a roof.

A bricklayer builds a fireplace and a chimney too.

A plumber puts in pipes for water.

An electrician wires
for electric lights.

Carpenters put in
windows and doors.

Painters paint
inside and out.

 56

The workers leave.

The house is built.

The family
moves inside.

57

Meet the Author and Illustrator

Byron Barton

Byron Barton became known as "the artist" in grade school. He got the name because he often painted pictures. He said, "My pictures were hanging all over the back walls of the class." He grew up to write and illustrate stories about how to do things like build a house, put together dinosaur bones, and travel on a spaceship.

READING: NARRATIVE ANALYSIS 3.3 Recollect, talk, and write about books read during the school year. HISTORY-SOCIAL SCIENCE 1.6.2 Identify the specialized work that people do to manufacture, transport, and market goods and services and the contributions of those who work in the home.

Theme Connections

Discuss

Within the Selection

1. Why does it take so many people to build a house?

2. Why must you build a house in a special order?

Across Selections

3. Would the steps in "Building a House" be used for all the houses in "Homes Around the World"? Why or why not?

Beyond the Selection

4. If you were building a house, which job would you enjoy?

Read

To learn more about homes being built, look for books or magazine articles to read on your own.

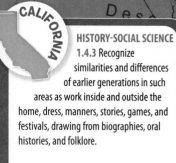

CALIFORNIA

HISTORY-SOCIAL SCIENCE
1.4.3 Recognize similarities and differences of earlier generations in such areas as work inside and outside the home, dress, manners, stories, games, and festivals, drawing from biographies, oral histories, and folklore.

Then and Now

Genre

Expository Text contains facts about real people and events.

Text Feature

Headings tell you what a paragraph will be about.

Long Ago

Long ago, people lived on farms. They grew their food. They raised animals to help them.

Their homes did not have electricity. They got heat from fireplaces. Life was not easy.

Now

Today's farms are different. Farmers still grow food. They still raise animals. Machines help farmers work. They make farmers' jobs easier.

City Life

Some people live in the city. Some people live in houses with a porch.

Homes can be big or small. Homes keep us safe.

1. How do you know that the first paragraph and the third paragraph are about different time periods?

2. Why might someone think it is easier to live on a farm now?

3. How do homes keep us safe?

CALIFORNIA WebLink

Visit **ImagineItReading.com/AtHome** for more information about living on farms.

Apply

Draw a picture of how farm life was long ago. Write a sentence about it.

CALIFORNIA

HISTORY-SOCIAL SCIENCE 1.3.3
Identify American symbols, landmarks, and essential documents, such as the flag, bald eagle, Statue of Liberty, U.S. Constitution, and Declaration of Independence, and know the people and events associated with them.

Read the article to find the meanings of:

- ✦ trudge
- ✦ president
- ✦ famous
- ✦ White House
- ✦ symbol
- ✦ address
- ✦ visit
- ✦ important

Vocabulary Development

Context Clues are hints in the text. They help you find the meaning of words. Look at the words *White House, president,* and *famous.* Use context clues to find each word's meaning.

Vocabulary

Warm-Up

I hear my brother Ben trudge down the steps. Ben doesn't know it is a special day. He doesn't know we are going to the White House.

"Come on!" I say. "We are going to visit 1600 Pennsylvania Avenue. That is the address of the White House!"

"Why is the White House important?" Ben asks. "We have seen lots of houses."

"The White House is a **symbol** of our country. The **president** lives in the White House," I tell Ben. "He's the leader of our country!"

"Is he **famous**?" Ben asks.

"Lots of people know him!" I say.

"You know what? I would like to get to know him too." Ben says.

Vocabulary Word Play

Use the vocabulary words to complete the following sentences.

On our class trip we will _____ the zoo.

The _____ is the leader of our country.

Concept Vocabulary

The concept word for this lesson is **lead.** To lead sometimes means "to be in charge of others." Your teacher leads your class. The president leads our country. Can you think of anyone else who leads? Explain your answer.

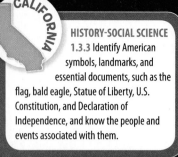

CALIFORNIA

HISTORY-SOCIAL SCIENCE
1.3.3 Identify American symbols, landmarks, and essential documents, such as the flag, bald eagle, Statue of Liberty, U.S. Constitution, and Declaration of Independence, and know the people and events associated with them.

Genre

Informational Writing informs or explains something real.

Comprehension Skill

☆ **Main Idea and Details**
Identify the main idea and details of the selection.

Focus Question

Why is the White House important?

The White House

by Lloyd G. Douglas

The White House has been a symbol of America for more than two hundred years.

The president of the United States lives in the White House with his family.

The address of the White House is 1600 Pennsylvania Avenue. It is in Washington, D.C.

Many presidents have lived in the White House.

John Adams was the first president to
live in the White House.

He was the second president of the United States.

The White House has many rooms.

The president works in a room called the Oval Office.

The East Room is the largest room in the White House.

Many parties and dinners have been held there.

People can visit some parts of the White House.

Many people visit the White House every year.

The White House is the most famous home in America.

It is an important American symbol.

Lloyd G. Douglas

Lloyd G. Douglas has written many selections. In his selections, he teaches children a lot about the United States. He has written books about the White House, the Statue of Liberty, the Pledge of Allegiance, and the American flag. Douglas writes books to help children understand more about themselves and the world around them.

CALIFORNIA

READING: NARRATIVE ANALYSIS 3.3 Recollect, talk, and write about books read during the school year. WRITING: ORGANIZATION AND FOCUS 1.2 Use descriptive words when writing. WRITING APPLICATIONS 2.2 Write brief expository descriptions of a real object, person, place, or event, using sensory details.

Theme Connections

Discuss

Within the Selection

1. Who lives in the White House?

2. What happens at the White House?

Across Selections

3. How is the White House different from other homes you have learned about in this unit?

Beyond the Selection

4. How is the White House a symbol?

Write

Describe a room in the White House. Write a sentence about it.

Read

To learn more about the White House, look for books or magazine articles to read on your own.

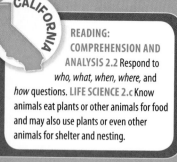
Genre

Poetry is a special
kind of writing in
which sounds and
meanings of words
are combined to
create ideas and
feelings.

Comprehension Strategy

☆ **Visualizing**
As you read,
picture in your mind
what is happening in
the selection.

Focus Question

What is the purpose
of a snail's shell?

Snail's Pace

by Aileen Fisher

illustrated by Pete Whitehead

Maybe it's so

that snails are slow.

They trudge along and tarry.

But isn't it true

you'd slow up, too,

if you had a house to carry?

82

Genre

Expository Text contains facts about real people and events.

Text Feature

Sequence is the order in which things are done.

Social Studies Link

Vote for the President!

There are rules for people who want to vote. First they must be United States citizens. They must be at least eighteen years old.

People who want to be president want people to vote for them. They talk to the press. They make speeches.

Presidents are elected. A president's job lasts for four years. Then there is another vote. Sometimes the president keeps his job. Other times someone else wins the vote. Members of our country vote for other leaders too.

1. What is the sequence of events in the third paragraph?

2. How long does a president keep the job?

3. Who votes for the president? Why do you think it is important to vote?

CALIFORNIA WebLink

Visit **ImagineItReading.com /AtHome** for more information about voting for president.

Apply

List any questions you have about the White House.

Read the article to find the meanings of:

✦ creatures
✦ hibernating
✦ place
✦ shady
✦ coat
✦ extra
✦ thaw
✦ belonging

Vocabulary Development

Apposition tells the definition of a word. Look at the word coat. The definition follows the word and is set off in commas.

Vocabulary

Warm-Up

Lots of creatures spend the winter hibernating. Bears hide away in the winter. They sleep in dens. Bears use plants to create a feeling of belonging in their dens. In the winter, bears may grow extra hair. This makes their coat, or fur, thick. It keeps them warm.

At the end of winter, the warm

weather of the thaw allows many plants to start to grow fruit. Bears eat things they can reach. They like berries. Bears also like nuts. Some bears will eat insects right out of their homes, or nests.

Bears are good swimmers. They move around in the morning and at night. They usually rest in a shady place, like a tree, during the hottest part of the day.

Vocabulary Word Web

Think about the word *belonging*. List examples of things that give you a feeling of belonging in your home.

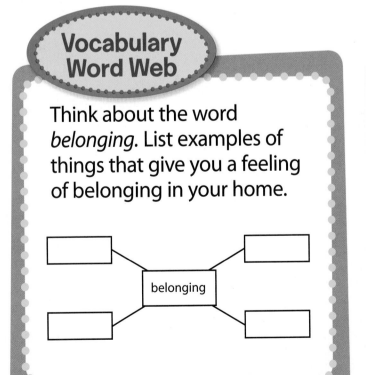

belonging

Concept Vocabulary

The concept word for this lesson is **dwelling**. A dwelling is a home. People live in many different dwellings. Some people live in houses. Others live in apartments. Can you think of any animal dwellings?

Finding

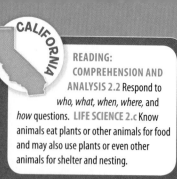

CALIFORNIA

READING: COMPREHENSION AND ANALYSIS 2.2 Respond to *who, what, when, where,* and *how* questions. **LIFE SCIENCE 2.c** Know animals eat plants or other animals for food and may also use plants or even other animals for shelter and nesting.

Genre

Informational Writing informs or explains something real.

Comprehension Sikll

☆ **Compare and Contrast**
As you read, compare and contrast ideas, characters, and events.

Focus Question
Where do animals live?

Shelter

by Daphne Butler

Whatever the Weather

What's the weather like where you live? Is it cold sometimes or rainy? Or is it very hot?

Almost all creatures, all over the world, need somewhere to shelter. Many must find shelter from the weather.

Warm Coats

Different animals have different
ways of living with the weather.

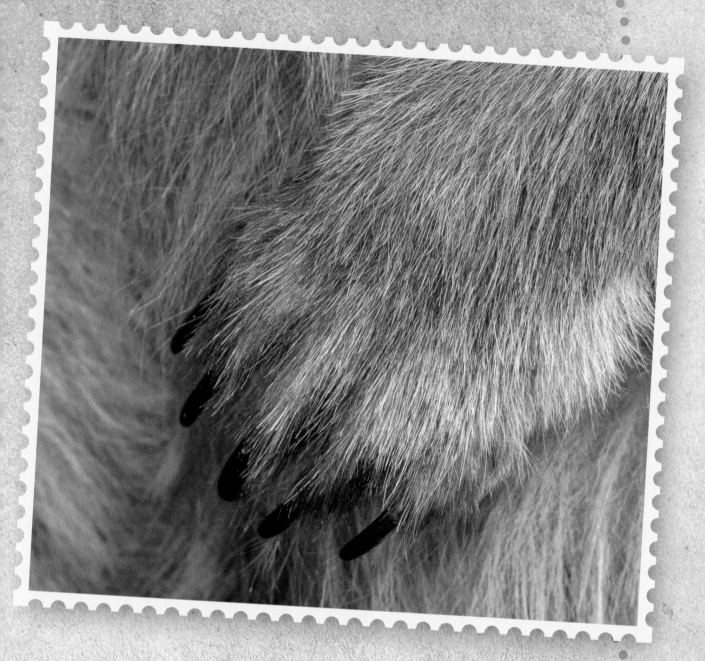

Some grow a thick hairy coat in autumn. This traps air, keeping their skin warm and dry.

The extra hair falls out in the spring. This leaves only a thin coat for the hot summer.

Sleeping until Spring

Some animals find a safe place to sleep in autumn. They stay there all winter, hibernating until spring. Then the weather warms up again.

Fish lie quietly on the bottom of
lakes and rivers. In the cold water
under ice, they wait for the thaw.

Shady Places

Animals in hot countries do not need thick coats. They need shady places. These shady covers protect them from the heat of the sun.

Some climb high in the leafy branches. Here they might find a cool breeze, too.

Safe Places

Animals also need safe places to hide from their enemies. This is a place their babies can stay until they are strong.

Holes in the Ground

Some animals dig themselves holes
in the ground. It is safe underground
and cool in summer, too.

A hole is a safe place to hibernate.
It keeps away the winter weather.

Nest Building

Some animals build nests.

Birds collect twigs, grass, or moss.
Wasps and hornets make theirs with
walls like paper.

How do you think spiders build their nests?

What kind of animals make strange-looking hills?

Building Houses

People also build nests to live in. They build houses with strong walls and roofs. Their houses are warm and dry in winter. They stay cool and shady in summer.

Living Anywhere

All animals, even people, learn how to live in the area around them.

People can also travel to any part of the world. They can change their clothes and their houses to go with the weather.

Meet the Author

Daphne Butler

Writing about all kinds of topics is Daphne Butler's specialty. She writes books to introduce students to interesting topics. She has written books about nature, the forest, and various animals. She has also written about places and objects, such as a hospital and wind.

READING: COMPREHENSION AND ANALYSIS 2.7 Retell the central ideas of simple expository or narrative passages. LIFE SCIENCE 2.c Know animals eat plants or other animals for food and may also use plants or even other animals for shelter and nesting.

Theme Connections

Discuss

Within the Selection

1. How do some animals stay warm in the winter?

2. Why do animals live in different kinds of homes?

Across Selections

3. How are animals' homes like the homes people live in?

Beyond the Selection

4. Think about animals that are not in the selection. What are their homes like?

Write

Why do animals and people need shelter?

Read

To learn more about animal homes, look for books or magazine articles about animal homes to read on your own.

READING:
COMPREHENSION AND
ANALYSIS 2.2 Respond to
who, what, when, where, and
how questions. 2.6 Relate prior knowledge
to textual information.

Genre

Poetry is a special kind of writing in which sounds and meanings of words are combined to create ideas and feelings.

Comprehension Strategy

Making Connections

As you read, make connections between what you know and what you are reading.

Focus Question

What do you think makes a good home?

Home

from *The Big Book of Classroom Poems*

by **Kathleen M. Hollenbeck**

illustrated by **Todd Bonita**

Home is more than
a bedroom and kitchen,
a place for your toothbrush,
a room with TV.
More than just shelter
from cold rainy weather,
home is a place
where you find family.
Home is a feeling,
a place of belonging.
No one can say
one is better or best.
Home is the place that your
heart wants to go to
when you need comfort,
    or laughter,
        or rest.

CALIFORNIA

READING: COMPREHENSION AND ANALYSIS 2.2 Respond to *who, what, when, where,* and *how* questions. **INVESTIGATION AND EXPERIMENTATION 4.d** Describe the relative position of objects by using two references (e.g., above and next to, below and left of).

Genre

Newspaper Articles tell about people, places, and things.

Text Feature

Quotes are statements made by people.

The Hope Town News
Animals Get a Drink
by Mary Myers

Some local people saw why lots of creatures live near Lake Hope.

"I have never seen so many deer in my life," said Roger Hand. "They were just to the right of the trees."

Susan Hand was just as excited. "We saw some raccoons under a bush," she said. "We even saw a turtle next to the lake. The hot day must have made the animals thirsty."

The Hands plan to come back to Lake Hope soon. "I hope we will see more animals!" said Mary Hand.

Perhaps that is why the lake is called Lake Hope.

1. What animal is to the right of the trees?

2. What place is this article about?

3. How can you tell what is said by Susan Hand?

WebLink

CALIFORNIA

Visit **ImagineItReading.com /AtHome** for more information about newspaper articles.

Apply

Look at a newspaper. Circle the quotes in one of the articles.

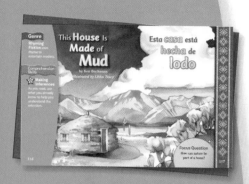

Read the article to find the meanings of:

- ✦ mice
- ✦ fence
- ✦ tunnels
- ✦ mud
- ✦ floor
- ✦ covered
- ✦ share
- ✦ visitors

Vocabulary Development

Word Analysis

Prefixes and suffixes can help you determine the meanings of words. The suffix *-ed* means "an action that is in the past." What does the word *share* mean? Use the meaning of the suffix *-ed* to determine the meaning of this word.

Vocabulary

Warm-Up

Mice are small hairy animals. They live in many areas. You may find mice living at the edge of a fence in a field. Many mice live in nests. Some live in nests under the ground. To live in underground nests, the mice dig tunnels through mud, or dirt. They make many rooms. Mice use tunnels to get from room to room.

To make their nests, mice use soft grass or plants. They line the floor, or bottom, of their nests. When the floor of the nest is covered, they make it soft. To do this, mice add a pile of tiny bits of soft grass. This makes a very soft bed.

Groups of mice can live in the same space. Mice share their space with each other. But mice do not like unknown visitors. They will stop strange mice from coming into their homes.

Vocabulary Word Play

Choose one vocabulary word, and write a few sentences about the word.

share Tell about a time when you shared something.

fence Where have you seen fences?

Concept Vocabulary

The concept word for this lesson is **divide**. To divide is to share a part of something. Sometimes we divide food. Other times we divide space. Can you think of something you have had to divide in your home?

115

Genre

Realistic Fiction is a make-believe story that could happen in the real world.

Comprehension Skills

 **Making Inferences**

As you read, use what you already know to help you understand the selection.

This House Is Made of Mud

by Ken Buchanan

illustrated by Libba Tracy

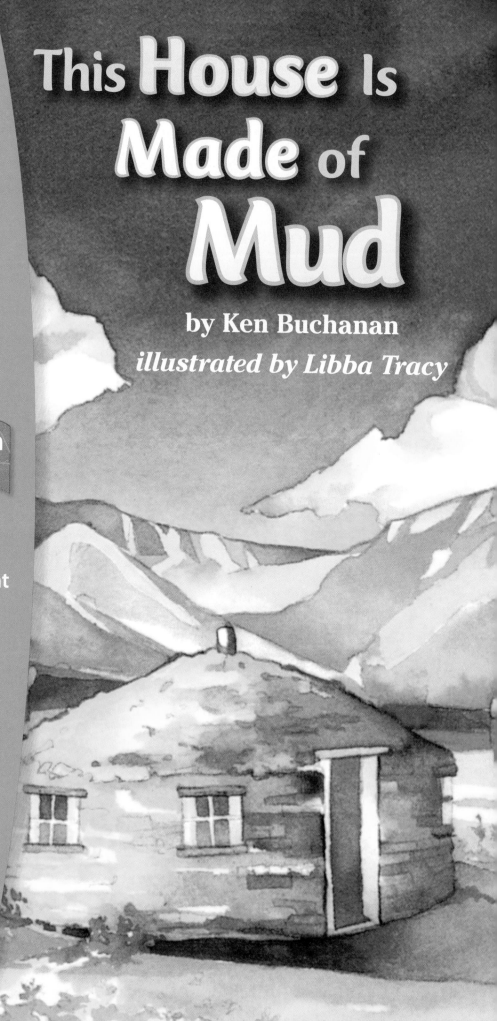

Esta casa está hecha de lodo

Focus Question

How can nature be
part of a home?

This house is made of Mud.

We made it, my Brothers and Sisters,
and Mother and Father.

We made this house from Earth, and
Water, and Straw.

We mixed them all together

And together made our Home.

This house is round, like the Earth,
and the Sun, and the Moon.

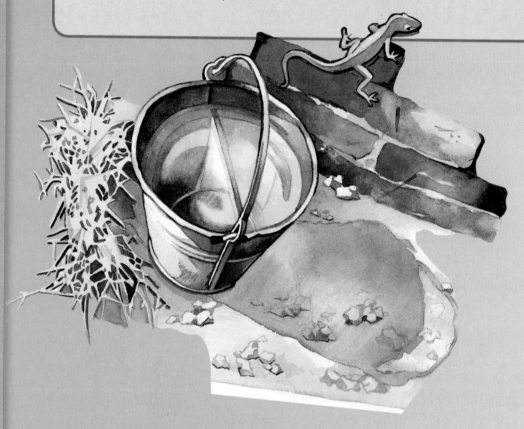

Esta casa está hecha de Lodo.

La hicimos, mis Hermanos y Hermanas,
y Mamá y Papá.

Hicimos esta casa de Tierra, de Agua y
de Paja.

Las mezclamos todas juntas
y juntos hicimos nuestro Hogar.

Esta casa es redonda, como la
Tierra, el Sol y la Luna.

It has only one door in and out.

But it has many windows so the breezes can pass through.

At night we can see the Stars,

And during the day, the Sky.

Tiene sólo una puerta para salir y entrar.

Pero tiene muchas ventanas por las cuales atraviesan las brisas.

✳

Por las noches podemos ver las Estrellas

Y durante el día, el Cielo.

We share our house with animals, large and small.

There are bugs that live in our walls.

There are mice that have tiny tunnels under our floor.

Compartimos nuestra casa con los animales, grandes y pequeños.

Hay bichitos que viven en nuestras paredes.

Hay ratoncitos que tienen pequeños túneles bajo nuestro piso.

There is my brother's dog, my sister's cat, my mother's bird, and baby brother's black snake.

He's only out at night, when we are asleep, and the mice are awake.

This house has a yard. It is round, too. We call it the Desert.

Hay, el perro de mi hermano, el gato de mi hermana, el pájaro de mi mamá y la culebra negra de mi hermanito.

La culebra sólo sale de noche, cuando estamos dormidos y los ratones están despiertos.

Esta casa tiene un jardín. También es redondo.

Lo llamamos el Desierto.

It has a fence around it. The fence is called the Mountains.

✳

Our yard, and our fence, are covered with plants—

From the giant cacti, to the smallest blades of grass.

Alrededor tiene una corralada. La corralada se llama las Montañas.

Nuestro jardín y nuestro muro, están cubiertos de plantas—

Desde el gigante cacto, hasta la hierba más pequeña.

Everyone has a name, but they are all
called Friends, because they share our yard.

We get many visitors to our house.

The Sun comes every day.

The Wind comes, but never stays.

Todos tienen un nombre, pero ellos se llaman
Amigos porque comparten nuestro jardín.

Llegan muchas visitas a nuestra casa.

El Sol llega todos los días.

El Viento llega pero nunca se queda.

129

The Rain's visit is not for long, just long enough for everyone to get a good drink.

La visita de la Lluvia no dura mucho, sólo lo suficiente para que todos beban un buen trago.

The snow sometimes falls. But the sun does not like the snow, and makes it go away.

This house was made of mud by our family. Made from the same thing our Earth is made of.

La nieve a veces cae. Pero al sol no le gusta la nieve y la hace que se vaya.

Esta casa fue hecha de lodo por nuestra familia. Hecha de la misma cosa de lo que está hecha nuestra Tierra.

Our house is shared by many, and many come to visit. They are all our Friends.

This house is our Home. And our home is made of Love.

Muchos comparten nuestra casa y muchos vienen a visitar. Todos son nuestros Amigos.

Esta casa es nuestro Hogar. Y nuestro hogar está hecho de Amor.

Meet the Author

Ken Buchanan

Ken Buchanan always dreamed of becoming an author. After many years of hard work, his dream finally came true. After Buchanan wrote this story, he and his family lived in their own mud house in the desert!

Meet the Illustrator

Libba Tracy

Libba Tracy has been a painter and an illustrator for a long time. Tracy gets ideas for her paintings by looking out her window, where she can see the mountains and the desert.

CALIFORNIA

READING: COMPREHENSION AND ANALYSIS 2.2 Respond to *who, what, when, where,* and *how* questions. NARRATIVE ANALYSIS 3.3 Recollect, talk, and write about books read during the school year. WRITING: ORGANIZATION AND FOCUS 1.2 Use descriptive words when writing.

Theme Connections

Discuss

Within the Selection

1. What material is the house made of?

2. Who are some of the visitors that live in the house?

Across Selections

3. How are the animals in "This House Is Made of Mud" similar to the animals in "Finding Shelter"?

Beyond the Selection

4. What makes a home special?

Write

Pretend you are building a house. What material will you use?

Read

To learn more about homes, look for books or magazine articles about homes to read on your own.

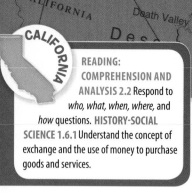

CALIFORNIA

READING: COMPREHENSION AND ANALYSIS 2.2 Respond to *who, what, when, where,* and *how* questions. **HISTORY-SOCIAL SCIENCE 1.6.1** Understand the concept of exchange and the use of money to purchase goods and services.

Genre

Newspaper Articles tell about people, places, and things that happen in nations, states, and cities.

Text Feature

Bylines tell who wrote the article.

A Home for Everyone

by Joan Taylor

Last week local kids helped build a house for their community. The house was for a family that did not have a home.

"Houses cost lots of money. We share the responsibility," said Rico. Rico's class sold fruit bars at sports games. "We made $900!" said Rico.

The money bought two doors for the house. Other kids earned money too. They washed cars. They pet sat. The kids thought about others. They knew people needed homes.

Some classes bought paint. Others bought shingles.

On Saturday the house was completed. It was good and sturdy.

1. Where do you find the byline? How does it help you?

2. How do the children get money to build the house?

3. Think about ways your class could earn money. Make a list.

CALIFORNIA WebLink

Visit **ImagineItReading.com /AtHome** for more information about earning money.

Apply

Look at different newspapers. Highlight or circle the byline.

Test-Taking Strategies

Test-Taking Strategy: Considering Every Answer Choice

Be sure to read all the answers to a question. You will not know whether an answer is correct unless you read it.

Considering Every Answer Choice

When you take a test, it is important that you carefully read every answer. Think about what the question is asking. Choose the answer that best answers the question.

Listen carefully to this question. Be sure to read all the answer choices.

A family went camping. Where do you think they slept?

○ in a house

○ in a room

○ in a tent

The important words in the question are *camping* and *slept.* You have to read all the answer choices to find the one that best answers the question. You can sleep in a house or in a room, but if you are camping, you will probably sleep in a tent.

The third answer is correct. Find the third answer, and point to the circle next to it.

Test-Taking Practice

Read the story below. Then complete the test on the next page.

Test Tip

Listen carefully to your teacher.

A Strange Home

The sunfish has a strange home. It is a hole in the bottom of a lake. The sunfish swims back and forth to make the hole. It has to do this many times.

The sunfish lays eggs in the hole. It protects the eggs. When they hatch, the babies stay near the hole. When they get big, they swim away.

Complete the test below.

1. What is the home of a sunfish?

○ rock

○ log

○ hole

2. How does the sunfish make its home?

○ by swimming back and forth

○ by digging with its fins

○ by using a tiny stick

3. Where do the baby sunfish stay?

○ in the weeds

○ near their home

○ in the sand

Test Tips

Read the question carefully.

Read each answer choice.

I Am Brave

Everyone is afraid of something. It is okay to have fears. Sometimes fears keep you safe. Sometimes you must face your fears.

Theme Connection

Look at the illustration. How do you think the boy in the illustration feels? How would you feel if you were on stage? Why would you feel that way? What could you do to face your fears?

Read the article to find the meanings of:

✦ underneath
✦ thinks
✦ scared
✦ beards
✦ clenched
✦ exciting
✦ pretended
✦ trembling

Vocabulary Development

Word Analysis

Prefixes and suffixes can help you determine the meanings of words. The suffix -ed means "an action that is in the past." What do the words clench and pretend mean? Use the meaning of the suffix -ed to determine the meanings of these words.

Vocabulary

Warm-Up

Joe wanted to go scuba diving. He loved the ocean. Joe wanted to see fish from underneath, or below, the surface of the water.

"Mom thinks I'm too young to scuba dive," said Joe.

"You're not too scared?" Joe's uncles laughed. They rubbed the beards on their faces.

Joe clenched his fists. He was tough. He wasn't afraid to scuba dive in the ocean.

"The ocean is an exciting place," said one uncle.

Joe's other uncle pretended to dive into the pool in Joe's yard. "Let's teach Joe here!" he said.

Then Joe understood. He could learn to dive in his pool this year.

Joe dived into the cold water. He was trembling when he got out. Joe was happy. His mom was happy too. Joe would be a safe diver.

Vocabulary Word Web

List six words or phrases you think of when you hear the word *scared*.

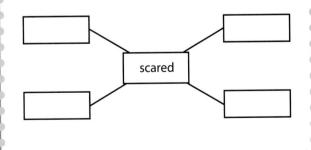

scared

Concept Vocabulary

The concept word for this lesson is **nervous.** To be nervous is to be easily upset or uneasy. Talk about what might make some people nervous. Do you think Joe's mom is nervous? Why?

CALIFORNIA

READING: COMPREHENSION AND ANALYSIS 2.2 Respond to *who, what, when, where,* and *how* questions.

Genre

Realistic Fiction is a make-believe story that could happen in the real world.

Comprehension Strategy

 Drawing Conclusions

As you read, use what you learn about the characters and events to help you better understand the selection.

My Brother Is AFRAID

# of Just About EVERYTHING

by Lois Osborn

illustrated by

Erica Pelton Villnave

My little brother is afraid of just about everything. Whenever there's a thunderstorm, I know where to find him.

Underneath the bed.

When we're outside and the mailman
comes, I know where to find him.
Behind the bushes.

He doesn't like men with beards.

When he's in the bathtub, he screams if I let the water out. Maybe he thinks he'll go down the drain along with the water.

So I take him out first. Then I empty the tub.

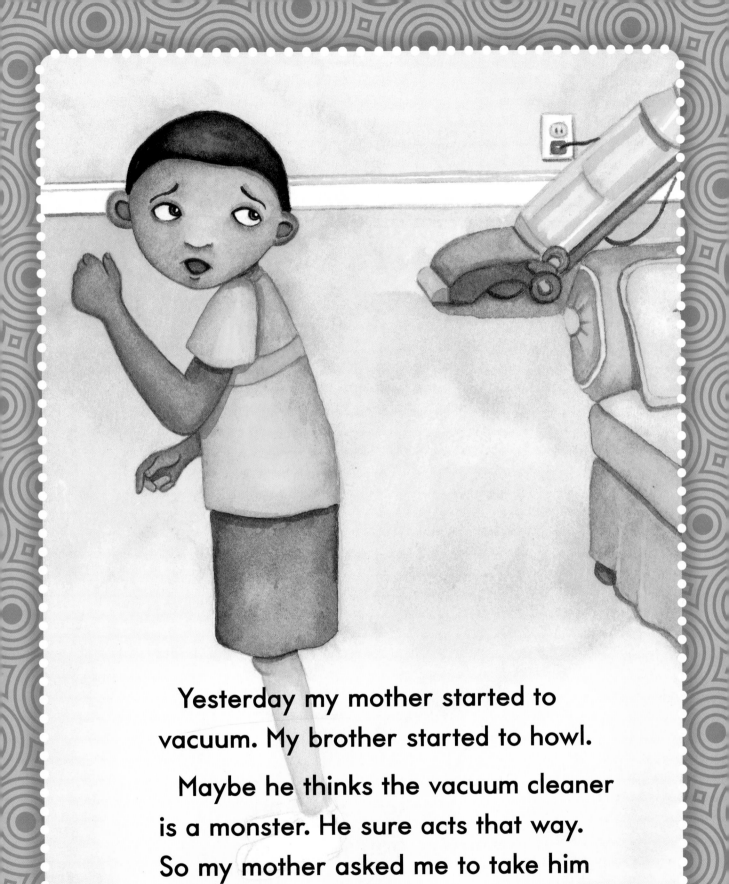

Yesterday my mother started to vacuum. My brother started to howl.

Maybe he thinks the vacuum cleaner is a monster. He sure acts that way. So my mother asked me to take him for a walk.

We went past my school. "See?" I said. "That's where you'll be going in a couple of years."

I could tell by my brother's face
what he thought about *that*.

We met some of my friends at the playground. They think my brother is cute. "What's your name?" and "How old are you?" they asked.

Did my brother answer them?
No-o-o, of course not.

He just buried his face in my
stomach, the way he always does.

On our way home, we came to some railroad tracks. A train was coming, so we waited to cross.

Most kids think trains are pretty exciting. They wave at the engineer. They count cars. But not my brother.

His arms went around me like boa constrictors. I couldn't have shaken him loose if I'd wanted to.

Back home, we sat together under the big tree in our backyard. I decided it was time we had a talk.

"Look," I said to him, "did thunder and lightning ever hurt you?" He shook his head.

"Or the mailman, or the vacuum cleaner?" He shook his head again.

"Then how come you're so scared of everything?" I asked.

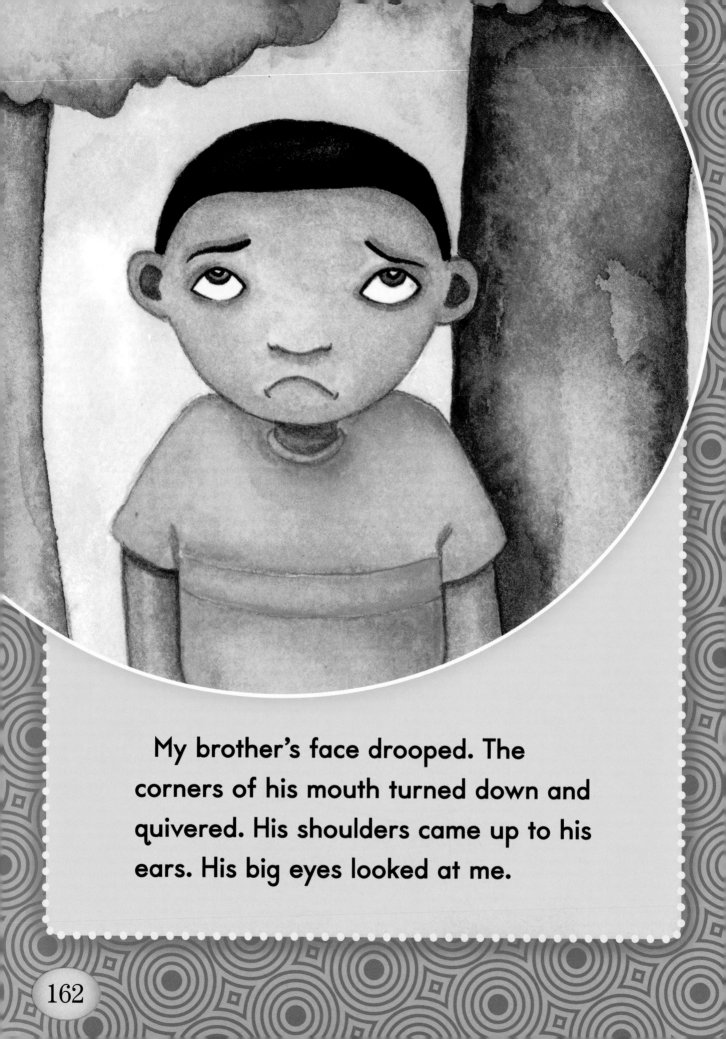

My brother's face drooped. The corners of his mouth turned down and quivered. His shoulders came up to his ears. His big eyes looked at me.

I felt like patting him on the back and saying that everything was okay.

But instead I said, "Look, you've got to get tough. It's stupid to keep on being afraid of things that won't hurt you."

Then I saw a great big, happy smile
spread across my brother's face. He
was looking at something behind me. I
didn't even have to ask what it was.

Nothing else could make my brother
look that happy. It had to be—a dog!

I tried. I tried very hard.

I shut my eyes and pretended the dog wasn't there.

I took deep breaths so my heart wouldn't beat so fast.

I clenched my hands so they would stop trembling.

I prayed the dog would go away.

Then I felt its feet upon my shoulders. I thought of sharp claws.

I felt its rough, wet tongue against the back of my neck. I thought of all those teeth.

That did it!

I couldn't get into the house fast enough!
Across the yard I ran. I yanked open the
screen door and quickly slammed it shut.
I even hooked it.

Safe behind the door, I stood, catching
my breath.

Then I went to the window. I knew what I would see.

Yes, there was my brother, with his arms around that dog.

I watched them play together.
I watched them for a long time.

I suppose that dog would have played with me, too, if I had been outside.

But I stayed inside.

I felt bad about it, but I stayed inside.

Oh well, everybody's afraid of something, I guess.

Meet the Author

Lois Osborn

For twenty-six years, Lois Osborn was a teacher. She started writing after she retired. She used to visit schools to read her books and talk about writing.

Meet the Illustrator

Erica Pelton Villnave

Inspiring children to read is a passion for Erica Pelton Villnave. She tries to create characters children can relate to. Villnave often uses watercolors to create her illustrations.

READING: COMPREHENSION AND ANALYSIS 2.2 Respond to *who, what, when, where,* and *how* questions. 2.3 Follow one-step written instructions. WRITING: WRITING APPLICATIONS 2.1 Write brief narratives e.g., fictional, autobiographical describing an experience. LISTEN/ SPEAK: SPEAKING APPLICATIONS 2.2 Retell stories using basic story grammar and relating the sequence of story events by answering *who, what, when, where, why,* and *how* questions.

Theme Connections

Discuss

Within the Selection

1. Why does the girl ask her brother if the vacuum cleaner has ever hurt him?

2. Why does the girl stay inside when her brother is playing with the dog?

Beyond the Selection

3. What things scare people?

4. How are people brave?

Write

Write a story about a time when someone was brave. The story could be about you.

Read

To learn more about people being brave, look for books or magazine articles about brave people to read on your own.

CALIFORNIA

READING: STRUCTURAL FEATURES OF INFORMATIONAL MATERIALS 2.1 Identify text that uses sequence or other logical order. INVESTIGATION AND EXPERIMENTATION 4.a Draw pictures that portray some features of the thing being described.

Social Studies Link

A Trip to the Ocean

Genre

Expository Text contains facts about real people and events.

Text Feature

Headings tell you what a paragraph will be about.

Take a Deep Look

The ocean is an exciting place. Some people scuba dive. They go deep underneath the surface of the water. They see lots of fish and plants.

Just Below

Other people snorkel. They put masks on their faces. They look into the water. They don't go deep.

The ocean can seem scary. There are many things to do near the ocean.

At the Beach

Some people collect shells. Others build sand castles. The boy in the picture thinks it is great fun to wade.

1. Make a list of fun activities that can be done by the ocean or in the ocean.

2. Tell why an activity from your list might seem scary to someone else.

3. Draw a picture of what you might see if you scuba dive.

WebLink

Visit **ImagineItReading.com /AtHome** for more information about the ocean.

Apply

Look for more ways to be safe and to have fun at the ocean.

CALIFORNIA

READING: VOCABULARY
AND CONCEPT
DEVELOPMENT 1.17
Classify grade-appropriate
categories of words (e.g., concrete
collections of animals, foods, toys).

Read the article to find the meanings of:

✦ solo
✦ thrill
✦ sly
✦ sneaking
✦ spooky
✦ shadows
✦ news
✦ booming

Vocabulary Development

Context Clues are hints in the text. They help you find the meanings of words. Look at the word *solo*. Use context clues to find the word's meaning.

Vocabulary
Warm-Up

Em loved to hear her mother play the piano. "I'm singing a solo at the talent show. I am going to sing alone on the stage," said Em. "Will you play the piano for me?"

"That would be a thrill for me!" said Em's mother with joy.

At the show Em was peeking around the curtain. She was trying to be sly. Em did not want the crowd to see her. Then she saw her mother sneaking onto the stage. It was time for her solo.

The lights went down in the gym. There was one bright light on Em as she stood on the stage. The rest of the stage was full of spooky shadows. It was very dark. Em was very nervous. "La la la," Em sang.

Soon the judges would decide the winner of the show. It seemed like forever before Em heard the news. The audience clapped when the winner was named. The crowd was booming with applause.

Vocabulary Word Web

Write six examples of things you have heard *booming*.

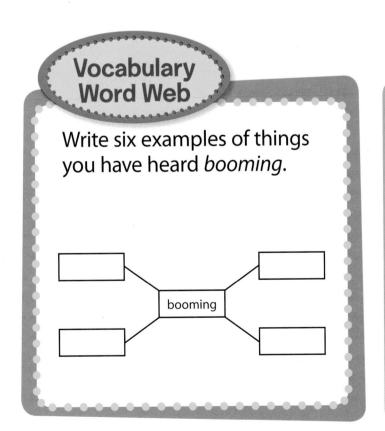

booming

Concept Vocabulary

The concept word for this lesson is **universe**. The universe is the sky, the stars, and everything in the world. You are a part of this universe. Explain what you can do to learn more about our universe.

CALIFORNIA

READING: COMPREHENSION AND ANALYSIS 2.2 Respond to *who, what, when, where,* and *how* questions. 2.7 Retell the central ideas of simple expository or narrative passages.

Genre

Realistic Fiction is a make-believe story that could happen in the real world.

Comprehension Strategy

☆ **Summarizing** As you read, use your own words to identify the important events or facts in the selection.

There's a BIG,

Focus Question

If you hide from scary things, what kinds of things will you miss?

Beautiful World Out There!

written and illustrated by
Nancy Carlson

There's a lot to be scared of, that's for sure!

There's that mean-looking dog,
and booming thunderstorms.

There are roller coasters,
and scary stories in the news.

There's a lot to be scared of, like
getting up in front of a whole bunch
of people, and spiders and other
creepy crawly things.

There are clowns, and spooky shadows in your room, and people who look different from you.

All this scary stuff can make you want to hide under your covers and never come out.

But after a while, hiding under your
covers can get pretty boring.

Maybe that scary dog only looks mean.

If you hide under your covers, you won't see the rainbow after the storm,

and you might never enjoy the thrill of
the ride!

If you hide under your covers, you'll miss your mother saying everything is going to be all right,

and you might never know how
great you sound singing a solo.

If you hide under your covers, you might not see all the interesting things in your own backyard.

You'll miss laughing out loud, and
you won't see the stars come out.

And just think of all the new friends you'll never meet!

There's a lot to be scared of, but there's even more to look forward to. . . .

So throw off those covers!

There's a big, beautiful world out there

just waiting for you!

Meet the Author and Illustrator

Nancy Carlson

Everyone should have fun, especially children. That is why Nancy Carlson's books are so much fun for children to read. Many of her stories are about important things that happened to her when she was young. She hopes that by writing and drawing about her challenges, children will understand they do not have to be perfect. Carlson likes to remember her favorite kind of book from her childhood as she creates illustrations for her books. If you guessed she liked comic books the best, then you were right!

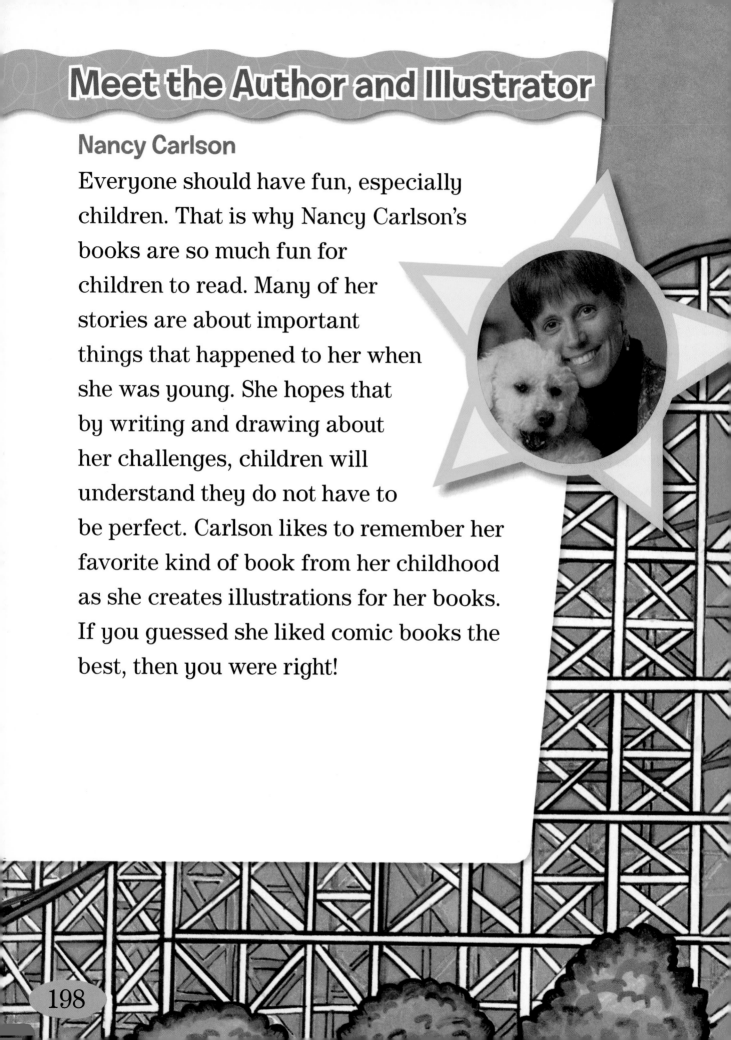

LISTEN/SPEAK: ORGANIZATION AND DELIVERY 1.5 Use descriptive words when speaking about people, places, things, and events. SPEAKING APPLICATIONS 2.2 Retell stories using basic story grammar and relating the sequence of story events by answering *who, what, when, where, why,* and *how* questions.

Theme Connections

Discuss

Within the Selection

1. What will you miss if you hide under your covers after a storm?

2. What interesting things are shown in the illustration of the backyard?

Across Selections

3. How is this selection like "My Brother Is Afraid of Just About Everything"?

Beyond the Selection

4. What makes you want to hide?

Write

Describe something exciting you would miss if you hid under your covers.

Read

To learn more about people being brave, look for books or magazine articles about brave people to read on your own.

199

READING: COMPREHENSION AND ANALYSIS 2.6 Relate prior knowledge to textual information.

Genre

Poetry is a special kind of writing in which sounds and meanings of words are combined to create ideas and feelings.

Comprehension Strategy

 Making Connections

As you read, make connections between what you know and what you are reading.

Focus Question

Why are some people afraid of the night?

Night Comes

by Beatrice Schenk de Regniers

illustrated by Emma Shaw-Smith

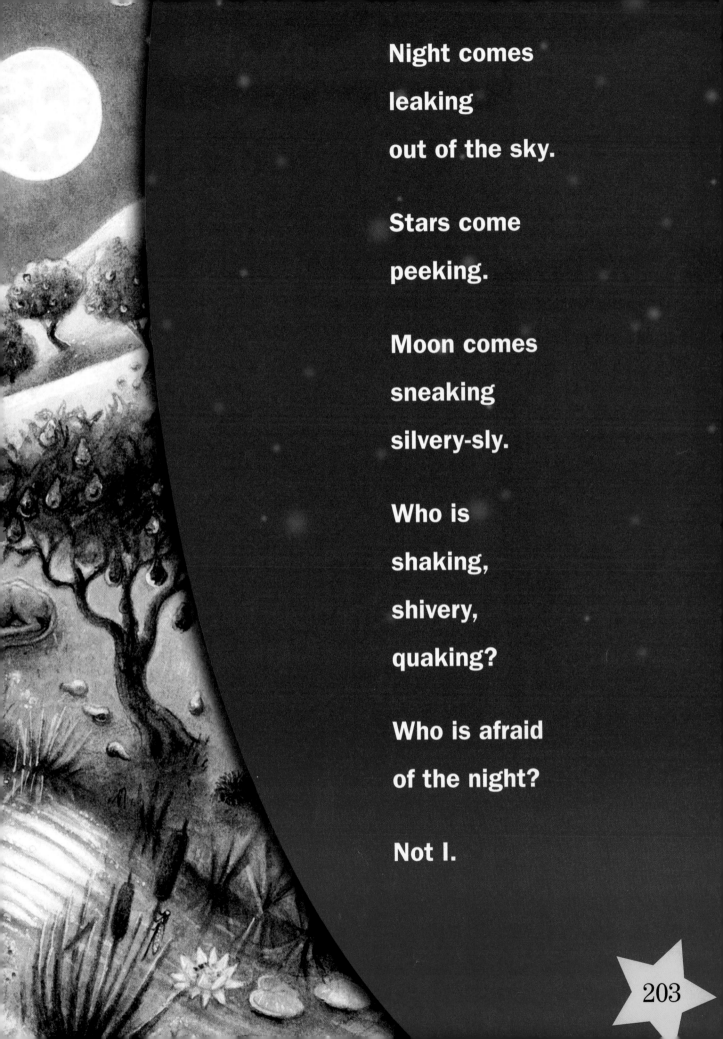

Night comes
leaking
out of the sky.

Stars come
peeking.

Moon comes
sneaking
silvery-sly.

Who is
shaking,
shivery,
quaking?

Who is afraid
of the night?

Not I.

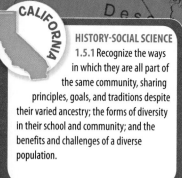
CALIFORNIA

HISTORY-SOCIAL SCIENCE
1.5.1 Recognize the ways in which they are all part of the same community, sharing principles, goals, and traditions despite their varied ancestry; the forms of diversity in their school and community; and the benefits and challenges of a diverse population.

Genre

Narrative Text is written from a first-person point of view. It is an account of personal events.

Text Feature

Sequence is the order in which things are done.

World Festival

Lucia is my friend. We go to the World Festival every year. We see customs from around the globe.

First we like to look at the clothes. We look at the kilts of Scotland. We also look at Kangas from Kenya. Kangas can be used as shawls. We choose our favorites. Then we try different foods. My favorite is nut soup. Lucia likes milk pie. Next we listen to music. Polka bands are our favorite. After that we try to do the dances. It is hard to learn the dances of so many cultures. It is great! What a thrill!

It is a long day! We learn about many cultures. We always have fun!

Think Link

1. What is the sequence of events at the World Festival?

2. Why do you think it might be hard to learn the dances?

3. Why do you think attending a World Festival would be fun?

CALIFORNIA **WebLink**

Visit **ImagineItReading.com /AtHome** for more information about world cultures.

Apply

Visit the library to find books about other culture.

CALIFORNIA

READING: VOCABULARY AND CONCEPT DEVELOPMENT 1.17 Classify grade-appropriate categories of words (e.g., concrete collections of animals, foods, toys).

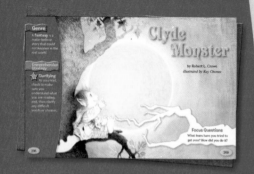

Read the article to find the meanings of:

+ clever
+ excitement
+ exclaimed
+ suggest
+ supposed to
+ clumsy
+ refused
+ trouble

Vocabulary Development

Apposition tells the definition of a word. Look at the word *suggest*. The definition follows the word and is set off by commas.

Vocabulary

Warm-Up

Mrs. Jones usually had clever students in class. The students wanted to start a class newspaper.

"There is so much excitement!" exclaimed Mrs. Jones. "Let me suggest, or give, some ideas. Make a list of jobs. Write who is supposed to do each job. Write ideas for stories."

The students had a lot to think about. They started to worry. The students could not be clumsy about this. But Mrs. Jones wasn't bothered. She refused to think bad

thoughts. Mrs. Jones could only smile. "Use the ideas I gave you. You won't have any trouble," pointed out Mrs. Jones.

The class worked together. The list they wrote helped. Everyone had a job. The students had lots of news to share!

Vocabulary Word Web

List four ways you could show *excitement*.

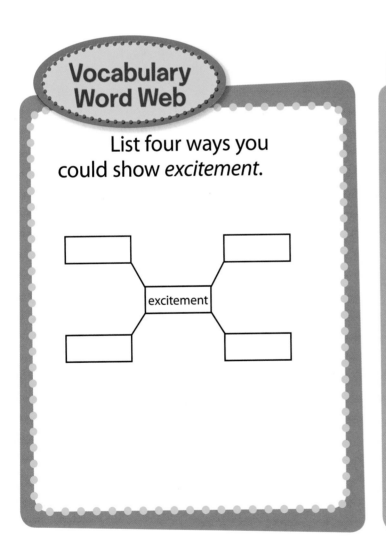

excitement

Concept Vocabulary

The concept word for this lesson is **worry.** To worry is to feel uneasy or upset.

Some people worry when they are late. Other people worry when they lose something. Talk about what makes you worry. Do you think everyone worries? Explain why.

CALIFORNIA

LISTEN/SPEAK: ORGANIZATION AND DELIVERY 1.5 Use descriptive words when speaking about people, places, things, and events . SPEAKING APPLICATIONS 2.3 Relate an important life event or personal experience in a simple sequence.

Genre

A **fantasy** is a make-believe story that could not happen in the real world.

Comprehension Strategy

 **Reality and Fantasy**

As you read, decide whether the characters and events are real or make-believe.

Clyde Monster

by Robert L. Crowe

illustrated by Kay Chorao

Focus Questions

What fears have you tried to get over? How did you do it?

Clyde wasn't very old, but he was
growing—uglier every day. He lived in
a large forest with his parents.

Father Monster was a big, big monster
and very ugly, which was good. Friends
and family usually make fun of a pretty
monster. Mother Monster was even uglier
and greatly admired. All in all, they were
a picture family—as monsters go.

Clyde lived in a cave. That is, he was supposed to live in a cave, at night anyway. During the day, he played in the forest, doing typical monster things like breathing fire at the lake to make the steam rise.

He also did typical Clyde things like turning somersaults that made large holes in the ground, and generally bumping into things. He was more clumsy than the average monster.

At night, Clyde was supposed to go
to his cave and sleep. That's when the
trouble started. He refused to go to
his cave.

"Why?" asked his mother. "Why won't
you go to your cave?"

"Because," answered Clyde, "I'm afraid
of the dark."

"Afraid," snorted his father until his nose burned. "A monster of mine afraid? What are you afraid of?"

"People," said Clyde. "I'm afraid there are people in there who will get me."

"That's silly," said his father. "Come, I'll show you." He breathed a huge burst of fire that lit up the cave. "There. Did you see any people?"

"No," answered Clyde. "But they may be hiding under a rock and they'll jump out and get me after I'm asleep."

"That is silly," pointed out his mother with her pointed tongue. "There are no people here. Besides, if there were, they wouldn't hurt you."

"They wouldn't?" asked Clyde.

"No," said his mother. "Would you ever hide in the dark under a bed or in a closet to scare a human boy or girl?"

"Of course not!" exclaimed Clyde, upset that his mother would even think of such a thing.

"Well, people won't hide and scare you either. A long time ago monsters and people made a deal," explained his father. "Monsters don't scare people, and people don't scare monsters."

"Are you sure?" Clyde asked.

"Absolutely," said his mother. "Do you know of a monster who was ever frightened by a people?"

"No," answered Clyde after some thought.

"Do you know of any boys or girls who were ever frightened by a monster?"

"No," he answered quickly.

"There!" said his mother. "Now off to bed."

"And no more nonsense about being scared by people," ordered his father.

"Okay," said Clyde as he stumbled into the cave. "But could you leave the rock open just a little?"

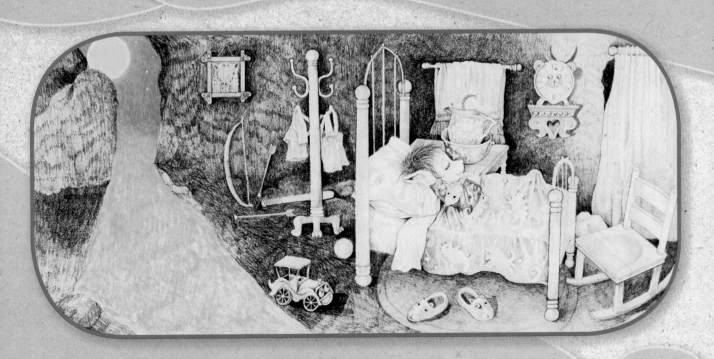

Meet the Author

Robert L. Crowe

School and children were familiar to Robert Crowe. Crowe used to be a teacher. Then he became a superintendent of schools. He wrote "Clyde Monster" to help his own children overcome their fear of the dark.

Meet the Illustrator

Kay Chorao

As a child, Kay Chorao loved to draw. As soon as she was old enough to hold a crayon, she "scribbled drawings over every surface," including the breakfast room table! Chorao is from Indiana. Now she lives in New York City.

CALIFORNIA

LISTEN/SPEAK: SPEAKING APPLICATIONS 2.2 Retell stories using basic story grammar and relating the sequence of story events by answering *who, what, when, where, why,* and *how* questions. 2.3 Relate an important life event or personal experience in a simple sequence.

Theme Connections

Discuss

Within the Selection

1. What is surprising about Clyde's fears?

2. How do you know that Clyde is still a little afraid at the end of the story?

Across Selections

3. How is "Clyde Monster" different from the poem "Night Comes"?

Beyond the Selection

4. How has another person helped you face your fears?

Write

Write words that describe how you feel when you are afraid.

Read

To learn more about being brave, look for books or magazine articles about being brave to read on your own.

READING: COMPREHENSION AND ANALYSIS 2.5 Confirm predictions about what will happen next in a text by identifying key words (i.e., signpost words).

Genre

A **fable** is a short story that teaches a lesson or moral.

Comprehension Strategy

☆ **Predicting** As you read, think about what will happen next in the selection. Confirm your predictions as you continue to read.

Focus Question

Why would a mouse want to stay away from a cat?

224

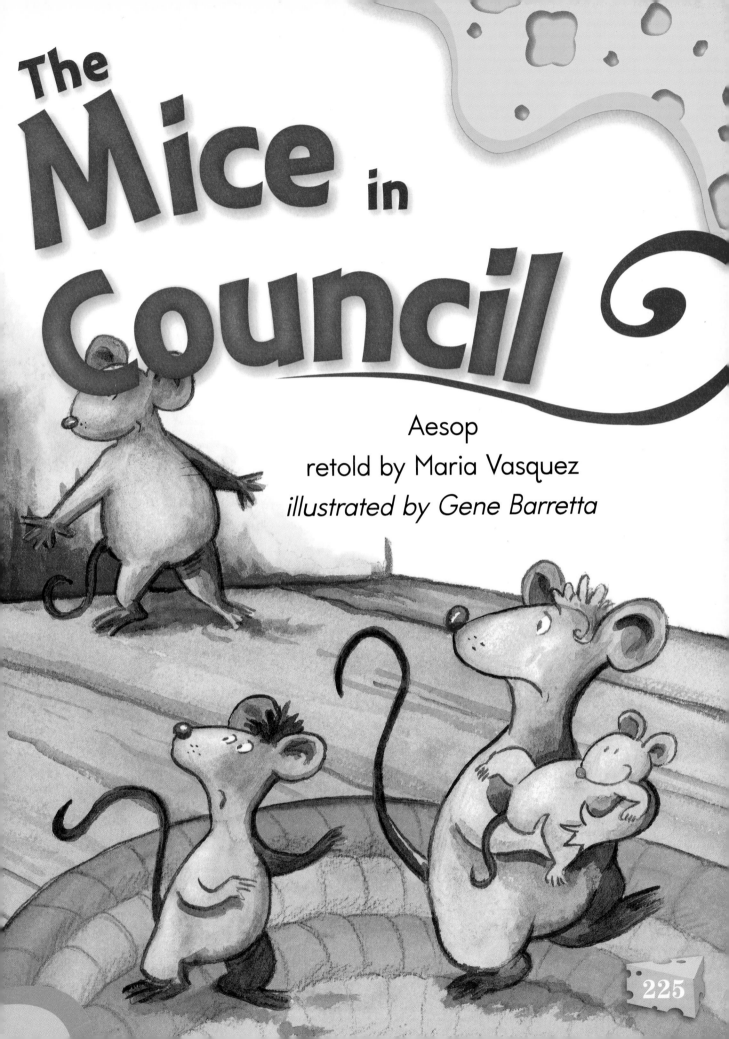

The Mice in Council

Aesop

retold by Maria Vasquez

illustrated by Gene Barretta

Once, a family of mice lived in a hole in a wall. Usually their days were filled with fun. Sometimes, though, things were not fun.

At times, the cat would appear. It was large and fierce. What a scary sight she was to the poor mice! The mice would have to run from the cat's sharp claws.

The mice called a meeting to suggest ways to stay safe from the cat. Several suggestions were discussed. Finally, a clever mouse yelled, "I think I have it! We can use a bell! We can hang it around the neck of the cat. The sound of the bell will warn us when she is coming near. Then we will have time to run and hide."

The mice squealed loudly. They all voted and agreed upon the idea with excitement.

Then a wise mouse stood up and said, "This is a great idea. But there is one flaw.

Meet the Author

Aesop

Aesop was a man who lived more than two thousand years ago. He liked to tell simple stories called fables. Aesop's fables usually have animals as characters and teach the reader a lesson.

Meet the Illustrator

Gene Barretta

Animals that behave like humans are Gene Barretta's favorite things to draw. Barretta enjoys visiting schools to talk to children about his books.

CALIFORNIA

LISTEN/SPEAK: SPEAKING APPLICATIONS 2.2 Retell stories using basic story grammar and relating the sequence of story events by answering *who, what, when, where, why,* and *how* questions. HISTORY-SOCIAL SCIENCE 1.1.1 Understand the rule-making process in a direct democracy (everyone votes on the rules) and in a representative democracy (an elected group of people makes the rules), giving examples of both systems in their classroom, school, and community.

Theme Connections

Discuss

Within the Selection

1. How would a bell protect the mice?

2. How does fear change the mice's plan?

Across Selections

3. How is the mouse family's fear different from Clyde Monster's fear?

4. How is the fable "The Mice in Council" similar to the story "Clyde Monster"?

Beyond the Selection

5. List examples of voting in your classroom, your school, and your community.

Write

Write a few sentences about what the mice could do to avoid the cat. Illustrate it.

Read

To learn more about people and animals facing fears, look for books or magazine articles to read on your own.

CALIFORNIA

READING: STRUCTURAL FEATURES OF INFORMATIONAL MATERIALS 2.1 Identify text that uses sequence or other logical order. **PHYSICAL SCIENCE 1.a** Know solids, liquids, and gases have different properties. **1.b** Know the properties of substances can change when the substances are mixed, cooled, or heated.

Genre

Informational Writing informs or explains something real.

Text Feature

Sequence is the order in which things are done.

Frozen Fruit Treats

You can make your own frozen treats! Always ask a grown-up for help when working in the kitchen. You might be afraid the recipe won't work. That's okay. If a grown-up helps, things usually turn out. You will need some fruit juice and an ice-cube tray. Then follow these steps:

1. Pour fruit juice into the tray.

2. Put the tray into the freezer.

3. Wait for a few hours or until the fruit juice is frozen.

4. Bend the tray to take out the frozen fruit cubes.

A drink is now a frozen treat!

BERRY

1. How is the sequence of steps helpful to you?

2. How can a fruit drink become a frozen treat?

3. The recipe says to wait a few hours. Explain why.

WebLink

CALIFORNIA

Visit **ImagineItReading.com /AtHome** for more information about solids, liquids, and gases.

Apply

Try this activity at home with a parent or an adult.

Read the article to find the meanings of:

- ✦ match
- ✦ plans
- ✦ office
- ✦ teddy bear
- ✦ goggles
- ✦ problem
- ✦ changed mind
- ✦ decided

Vocabulary Development

Context Clues are hints in the text. They help you find the meanings of words. Look at the word *goggles*. Use context clues to find the word's meaning.

Vocabulary

Warm-Up

After I won my chess match, Mom had great news. She made plans to take me to her office. I will learn what my mom does at work. I can bring my teddy bear, but I'm not going to. I want to look like a grown-up.

Mom works with big machines. My dreams used to be haunted by those big machines. Mom agrees machines can be kind of scary!

But she works safely. Mom wears goggles to keep her eyes safe. And if there is a problem, she can fix it.

I changed my mind. I will bring my teddy bear. I'm not scared—I decided that I want my teddy bear to see the cool things my mom does at work.

Vocabulary Word Play

Choose one vocabulary word listed below, and answer the question next to the word.

changed mind Have you ever changed your mind about something?

office Have you ever visited an office?

Concept Vocabulary

The concept word for this lesson is **comfort.** Comfort is offered or given when someone is frightened or uneasy. Talk about why all people need comfort at one time or another. Why might comfort be important?

Ira

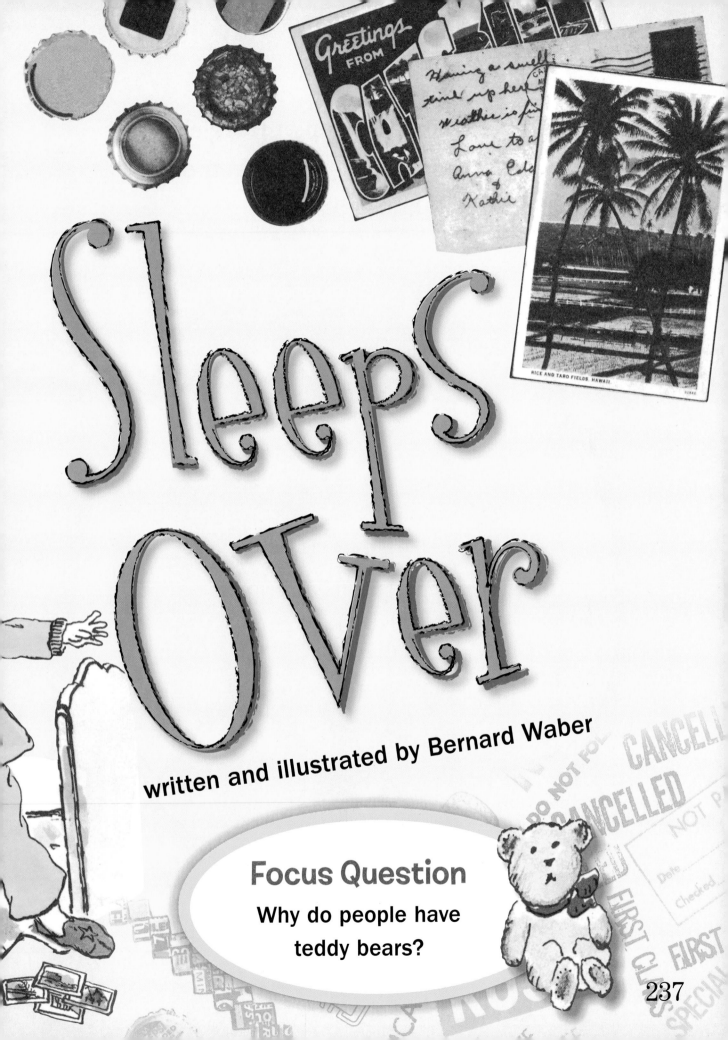

Sleeps Over

written and illustrated by Bernard Waber

Focus Question

Why do people have
teddy bears?

I was invited to sleep at Reggie's
house. Was I happy! I had never slept
at a friend's house before.

But I had a problem. It began when my
sister said: "Are you taking your teddy
bear along?"

"Taking my teddy bear along!" I said.
"To my friend's house? Are you kidding?
That's the silliest thing I ever heard! Of
course, I'm not taking my teddy bear."

And then she said: "But you never
slept without your teddy bear before.
How will you feel sleeping without
your teddy bear for the very first time?
Hmmmmmmm?"

"I'll feel fine. I'll feel great. I will probably love sleeping without my teddy bear. Just don't worry about it," I said.

"Who's worried?" she said.

But now, she had me thinking about it.
Now, she really had me thinking about it.
I began to wonder: Suppose I won't like
sleeping without my teddy bear. Suppose
I just hate sleeping without my teddy
bear. Should I take him?

"Take him," said my mother.

"Take him," said my father.

"But Reggie will laugh," I said.
"He'll say I'm a baby."

"He won't laugh," said my mother.

"He won't laugh," said my father.

"He'll laugh," said my sister.

I decided not to take my teddy bear.

That afternoon, I played with Reggie. Reggie had plans, big plans. "Tonight," he said, "when you come to my house, we are going to have fun, fun, fun. First, I'll show you my junk collection. And after that we'll have a wrestling match. And after that, a pillow fight.

"And after that we'll do magic tricks. And after that we'll play checkers. And after that we'll play dominoes. And after that we can fool around with my magnifying glass."

"Great!" I said. "I can hardly wait. By the way," I asked, "what do you think of teddy bears?"

But Reggie just went on talking
and planning as if he had never
heard of teddy bears. "And after
that," he said, "do you know what
we can do after that—I mean when
the lights are out and the house
is really dark? Guess what we
can do?"

"What?" I asked.

"We can tell ghost stories."

"Ghost stories?" I said.

"Ghost stories," said Reggie, "scary, creepy, spooky ghost stories."

I began to think about my teddy bear.

"Does your house get very dark?" I asked.

"Uh-huh," said Reggie.

"Very, very dark?"

"Uh-huh," said Reggie.

"By the way," I said again, "what do you think of teddy bears?"

Suddenly, Reggie was in a big hurry to go someplace. "See you tonight," he said.

"See you," I said.

I decided to take my teddy bear.

"Good," said my mother.

"Good," said my father.

But my sister said: "What if Reggie
wants to know your teddy bear's name.
Did you think about that? And did you
think about how he will laugh and say
Tah Tah is a silly, baby name, even for a
teddy bear?"

"He won't ask," I said.

"He'll ask," she said.

I decided not to take my teddy bear.

At last, it was time to go to Reggie's house.

"Good night," said my mother.

"Good night," said my father.

"Sleep tight," said my sister.

I went next door where Reggie lived.

DUPLICATE DUPLICATE DUPLICATE

FIRST CLASS
SPECIAL DELIVERY

THIS SIDE UP

That night, Reggie showed me his junk. He showed me his flashlight, his collection of bottle caps, a chain made of chewing gum wrappers, some picture postcards, an egg timer, jumbo goggles, a false nose and mustache, and a bunch of old rubber stamps and labels from his father's office. We decided to play "office" with the rubber stamps.

After that we had a wrestling match.

And after that we had a pillow fight.

And after that Reggie's father said:

"Bedtime!"

"Already?" said Reggie.

"Already," said his father.

We got into bed.

"Good night," said Reggie's father.

"Good night," we said.

Reggie sighed.

I sighed.

"We can still tell ghost stories," said Reggie.

"Do you know any?" I asked.

"Uh-huh," said Reggie.

Reggie began to tell a ghost story:

"Once there was this ghost and he lived in a haunted house only he did most of the haunting himself. This house was empty except for this ghost because nobody wanted to go near this house, they were so afraid of this ghost.

And every night this ghost would walk
around this house and make all kinds of
clunky, creeky sounds. *Aroomp! Aroomp!*
Like that. And he would go around
looking for people to scare because
that's what he liked most to do: scare
people. And he was very scary to look at.
Oh, was he scary to look at!"

Reggie stopped. "Are you scared?"
he asked.

"Uh-huh," I said. "Are you?"

"What?" said Reggie.

"Are you scared?"

"Just a minute," said Reggie, "I have
to get something."

"What do you have to get?" I asked.

"Oh, something," said Reggie.

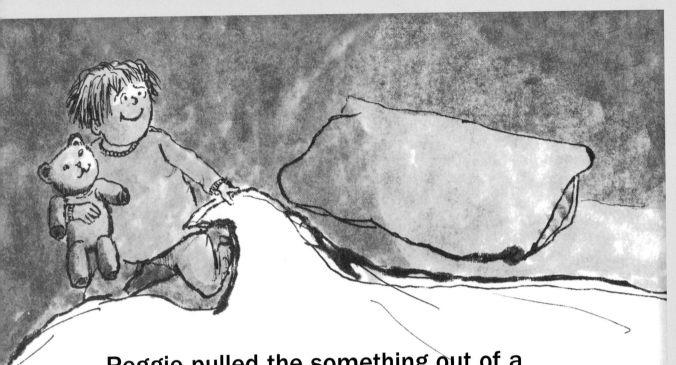

Reggie pulled the something out of a drawer. The room was dark, but I could see it had fuzzy arms and legs and was about the size of a teddy bear. I looked again. It was a teddy bear.

Reggie got back into bed. "Now, about this ghost . . ." he said.

"Is that your teddy bear?" I asked.

"What?" said Reggie.

"Is that your teddy bear?"

"You mean this teddy bear?"

"The one you're holding," I said.

"Uh-huh," Reggie answered.

"Do you sleep with him all of the time?"

"What?" said Reggie.

"Do you sleep with him all of the time?"

"Uh-huh."

"Does your teddy bear have a name? Does your teddy bear have a name?" I said louder.

"Uh-huh," Reggie answered.

"What is it?"

"You won't laugh?" said Reggie.

"No, I won't laugh," I said.

"Promise?"

"I promise."

"It's Foo Foo."

"Did you say 'Foo Foo'?"

"Uh-huh," said Reggie.

"Just a minute," I said, "I have to get something."

"What do you have to get?" Reggie asked.

"Oh, something," I answered.

The next minute, I was ringing my own doorbell. The door opened.

"Ira!" everyone said. "What are you doing here?"

"I changed my mind," I answered.

"You what!" said my mother.

"You what!" said my father.

"You what!" said my sister.
(She was still up.)

"I changed my mind," I said. "I decided to take Tah Tah after all."

I went upstairs. Soon, I was down again with Tah Tah.

My sister said: "Reggie will laugh. You'll see how he'll laugh. He's just going to fall down laughing."

"He won't laugh," said my mother.

"He won't laugh," said my father.

"He won't laugh," I said.

I came back to Reggie's room. "I have
a teddy bear, too," I said. "Do you want
to know his name?" I waited for Reggie
to say, Uh-huh. But Reggie didn't say,
Uh-huh. Reggie didn't say anything. I
looked at Reggie. He was fast asleep.
Just like that, he had fallen asleep.

"Reggie! Wake up!" I said. "You have to finish telling the ghost story." But Reggie just held his teddy bear closer and went right on sleeping. And after that—well, there wasn't anything to do after that. "Good night," I whispered to Tah Tah. And I fell asleep, too.

Meet the Author and Illustrator

Bernard Waber

Writing about family problems is something Bernard Waber loves to do. Waber uses funny characters to tell about things that might happen to you or me. He is best known for his books about a crocodile named Lyle. Waber's funny illustrations make children and grown-ups laugh out loud!

CALIFORNIA

LISTEN/SPEAK: SPEAKING APPLICATIONS **2.2** Retell stories using basic story grammar and relating the sequence of story events by answering *who, what, when, where, why,* and *how* questions. **2.3** Relate an important life event or personal experience in a simple sequence.

Theme Connections

Discuss

Within the Selection

1. Why is Ira worried about taking his teddy bear to Reggie's house?

2. What changes the way Ira feels?

Across Selections

3. How is this story similar to "My Brother Is Afraid of Just About Everything"?

Beyond the Selection

4. How have you helped someone who was afraid?

Write

Write a few sentences about a time when you stayed at a friend's or relative's house.

Read

To learn more about people facing fears, look for books or magazine articles to read on your own.

Social Studies Link

What Will You Be?

There are all kinds of jobs. What will you be when you grow up?

Outdoors

Some people like to work outdoors. Mail carriers work outside. Park rangers work outside too.

Builders

Some people like to build. Carpenters build. So do construction workers. They build houses, offices, and even schools.

Animal Lovers

People who work at a zoo or as a vet love animals. They might solve an animal's health problem.

Watch people who work in your city. What will you be?

Genre

Expository Text contains facts about real people and events.

Text Feature

Headings tell you what a paragraph will be about.

1. How is the heading for the third paragraph helpful?

2. Why might someone who likes to work outside consider a job as a mail carrier?

3. Some people love animals. Explain why the zoo might be a good place for them to work.

CALIFORNIA WebLink

Visit **ImagineItReading.com /AtHome** for more information about jobs.

Apply

Watch people working at school or in your community. Write about the jobs you like.

Test-Taking Strategy: Referring to a Story to Answer Questions

To answer some questions on a test, you will have to read a story. You must use the information in the story to answer the questions.

Referring to a Story to Answer Questions

Sometimes you will read a story on a test. You will have to answer questions about the story. It is important that you use the information in the story to answer the questions.

Listen carefully as this story is read. Follow along, and think about the story as you listen.

Nick is a big brown dog. He has floppy ears. Nick likes to chase a ball. If you throw the ball, he will run after it. Then he will bring it back.

Listen carefully to the question.

> What color is Nick?
>
> ○ brown
>
> ○ gray
>
> ○ white

Look back at the story. The first sentence is *Nick is a big brown dog.* This tells you the answer. The story says Nick is a *brown* dog. Find the first answer, and point to the circle next to it.

Test-Taking Practice

Read the story below. Then complete the test on the next page.

First Ride

"Just ride like you always do," said Dad. "Let's go!"

Kerry was a little afraid. Even so, she started pedaling. Mom was down the street in front of the house. Kerry felt Dad let go of the bike. She did not fall.

Mom was clapping. Kerry kept pedaling. She was doing it! When she got close to Mom, she put on the brakes and stopped.

"Mom, I did it!" Kerry got off the bike and gave Mom a hug. Then Kerry got back on the bike and rode back to Dad.

Complete the test below.

1. Kerry was riding a

○ wagon.

○ sled.

○ bike.

2. Who was clapping?

○ Mom

○ Dad

○ Kerry

3. At the end of the story, Kerry

○ ran to Mom.

○ rode back to Dad.

○ went into the house.

Test Tip

Use the story to answer the questions or complete the sentences.

Test Tips

Read each answer choice. Look back at the story if you are not sure.

Pronunciation Key

a as in **a**t
ā as in l**a**te
â as in c**a**re
ä as in f**a**ther
e as in s**e**t
ē as in m**e**
i as in **i**t
ī as in k**i**te
o as in **o**x
ō as in r**o**se

ô as in b**o**ught and r**a**w
oi as in c**oi**n
o͞o as in b**oo**k
o͞o as in t**oo**
or as in f**or**m
ou as in **ou**t
u as in **u**p
ū as in **u**se
ûr as in t**ur**n, g**er**m, l**ear**n, f**ir**m, w**or**k

ə as in **a**bout, chick**e**n, penc**i**l, cann**o**n, circ**u**s
ch as in **ch**air
hw as in **wh**ich
ng as in ri**ng**
sh as in **sh**op
th as in **th**in
t͟h as in **th**ere
zh as in trea**s**ure

The mark (ˊ) is placed after a syllable with a heavy accent, as in **chicken** (**chik**ˊ ən).

The mark (ˎ) after a syllable shows a lighter accent, as in **disappear** (**dis**ˊ ə **pēr**ˊ).

Glossary

A

absolutely (ab´ sə lo͞ot´ lē) *adv.* Certainly; without a doubt.

address (ad´ res) *n.* A building number that helps to find a house or business on a street.

America (ə mer´ i kə) *n.* A shortened name for the United States of America.

Arctic (ärk´ tik) *n.* Area around the North Pole where it is very cold and freezing year-round.

area (âr´ ē ə) *n.* Part of a town, city, country, or the world.

at hand (at hand) *adv.* Within reach.

autumn (ô´ təm) *n.* The season between summer and winter; fall.

average (av´ ər ij) *adj.* Usual; not different from others.

B

baked (bākt) *adj.* Hardened by heating.

beards (bērdz) *n.* Plural of **beard:** The hair that grows on a man's face.

belonging (bi lông´ ing) *v.* Having a close connection with others.

blankets (blang´ kits) *n.* Plural of **blanket:** A cover used to keep warm.

Pronunciation Key: at; lāte; câre; fäther; set; mē; it; kīte; ox; rōse; ô in bought; coin; bo͞ok; toͦo; form; out; up; ūse; tûrn; ə sound in about, chicken, pencil, cannon, circus; chair; hw in which; ring; shop; thin; there; zh in treasure.

blocks (bloks) *n.* Plural of **block:** A hard, solid brick usually made from cement or concrete used for building houses.

booming (bo͞om ing) *v.* Making a deep, loud sound.

boring (bôr´ ing) *adj.* Not exciting or fun.

bricklayers (brik´ lā ərz) *n.* Plural of **bricklayer:** A person who builds walls using bricks or concrete blocks.

builders (bil´ dərz) *n.* Plural of **builder:** One who builds or makes things, such as houses.

bulldozer (bo͞ol´ dō´ zər) *n.* A large powerful machine used to move dirt, stones, and trees.

bulldozer

bunch (bunch) *n.* A group of something.

buried (ber´ ēd) *v.* Past tense of **bury:** To hide, cover up.

C

cacti (kak´ tī) *n.* Plural of **cactus:** A desert plant.

cactus

carpenters (kär´ pən tərz) *n.* Plural of **carpenter:** A person who makes things out of wood.

cement (si ment´) *n.* A mix of sand, water, and rock that dries as hard as stone.

changed mind (chānjd mīnd) *v.* Past tense of **change mind:** To go back on a decision.

chimney (chim´ nē) *n.* The part of a house that carries smoke away from a fireplace or furnace to the outdoors.

clay (klā) *n.* Soft, sticky mud.

clenched (klencht) *v.* Past tense of **clench:** To close tightly.

clever (klev´ ər) *adj.* Very smart.

clumsy (klum´ zē) *adj.* Awkward; not graceful.

clumsy

coat (kōt) *n.* The fur covering of an animal.

covered (kuv´ ərd) *adj.* Hidden.

covers (kuv´ ərz) *n.*
Plural of **cover:** The
sheets and blankets
used on a bed.

creatures (krē´ chərz)
n. Plural of **creature:** A
living person or animal.

D

deal (dēl) *n.* An
agreement.

decided (di sī´ ded) *v.*
Past tense of **decide:**
To make up your mind.

drain (drān) *n.* An
opening or pipe that
takes liquid out of
something.

drawer (drôr) *n.* A box
that fits inside a piece
of furniture that can be
pulled out and pushed in.

drooped (droopt) *v.* Past
tense of **droop:** To hang
or sink down.

East Room (ēst room) *n.*
The largest room in the
White House.

electrician (i lek trish´
ən) *n.* A person who
works with wires and
electricity.

empty (emp´ tē) *v.* To
remove all that is in
something.

enemies (en´ ə mēz)
n. Plural of **enemy:** A
person or animal that
wants to hurt another.

excitement (ik sīt´ mənt) *n.* A mood or feeling of high interest or energy; delight; joy.

exciting (ik sī´ ting) *adj.* Very interesting.

exclaimed (ik sklāmd´) *v.* Past tense of **exclaim:** To speak out suddenly and loudly.

extra (ek´ strə) *adj.* More than is needed.

famous (fā´ məs) *adj.* Very well known.

feeling (fē´ ling) *n.* An emotion; sadness, joy, fear, and anger are feelings.

fence (fens) *n.* Something used to border, protect, or surround an area.

fence

flaw (flô) *n.* A problem or defect.

floor (flôr) *n.* The area of a room that people walk or stand on.

fold (fōld) *v.* To bend in sections.

goggles (gog´ əlz) *n.* Protective glasses.

goggles

Pronunciation Key: at; l**ā**te; c**â**re; f**ä**ther; s**e**t; m**ē**; **i**t; k**ī**te; **o**x; r**ō**se; **ô** in b**o**ught; c**oi**n; b**oo**k; t**oo**; f**o**rm; **ou**t; **u**p; **ū**se; t**û**rn; **ə** sound in **a**bout, chick**e**n, penc**i**l, cann**o**n, circ**u**s; **ch**air; **hw** in **wh**ich; ri**ng**; **sh**op; **th**in; **th**ere; **zh** in trea**s**ure.

H

hibernating (hī´ bər nāt´ ing) *v.* Sleeping through winter.

home (hōm) *n.* A place people live.

howl (houl) *v.* To let out a loud cry.

hut (hut) *n.* A small plain house.

I

important (im pôr´ tənt) *adj.* Having great value or meaning.

invited (in vīt´ id) *v.* Past tense of **invite:** To ask someone to go somewhere.

K

kidding (kid´ ing) *v.* Teasing, saying something that is not true to be funny.

kitchen (kich´ ən) *n.* A room in a house where people cook food and make meals.

L

lakes (lāks) *n.* Plural of **lake:** A body of water surrounded by land.

leaking (lēk´ ing) *v.* Coming out slowly.

M

magnifying glass (mag´ nə fī´ ing glas) *n.* A piece of glass that makes things look bigger.

magnifying glass

match (mach) *n.* A contest or game.

mice (mīs) *n.* Plural of **mouse:** A small, furry animal with a pointed nose, small ears, and a long, thin tail.

mixed (mikst) *v.* Past tense of **mix:** To combine two or more things together; to blend.

mud (mud) *n.* Soft, wet, and heavy dirt or earth.

N

never (nev´ ər) *adv.* Not ever; not at any time.

news (nooz) *n.* A report of information on something that just happened.

O

office (ô´ fis) *n.* A place businesspeople work.

Oval Office (ō´ vəl ô´ fis) *n.* The room in the white house where the president works.

P

packed (pakt) *adj.* Pressed or squeezed together.

place (plās) *n.* Where something is; where something happens.

plans (planz) *n.* Plural of **plan:** An idea for doing something that is thought out ahead of time.

plumber (plum´ ər) *n.* A person who fixes and puts together water pipes.

pointed out (poin´ ted out) *v.* Past tense of **point out:** To explain.

porch (pôrch) *n.* An entrance covered with a roof.

porch

president (prez´ i dənt) *n.* The leader of the United States.

pretended (pri ten´ ded) *v.* Past tense of **pretend:** To make believe.

problem (prob´ ləm) *n.* A personal difficulty; a tricky or uncomfortable situation.

pueblo (pweb´ lō) *n.* A group of houses built on top of each other, made of stone or adobe bricks.

pueblo

Q

quaking (kwāk´ ing) *v.* Shaking or trembling.

R

refused (ri fūzd´) *v.* Past tense of **refuse**: To turn down or say no.

roof (rōōf) *n.* The outer covering of the top of a house or building.

S

safe (sāf) *adj.* Protected from danger.

saw (sô) *v.* To move a sharp blade back and forth to cut wood.

scared (skârd) *adj.* Frightened or afraid.

shadows (shad´ ōz) *n.* Plural of **shadow**: Area of darkness where there is little or no light.

shadow

shady (shā´ dē) *adj.* Giving shade; blocking out light.

share (shâr) *v.* To use something together; to divide equally.

shelter (shel´ tər) *n.* Something that covers or protects.

shivery (shiv´ ər ē) *adj.* Describes someone who is shaking because of cold or fear.

silliest (sil´ ē est) *adj.* Funniest or most foolish.

simple (sim´ pəl) *adj.* Plain.

Pronunciation Key: at; l**ā**te; c**â**re; f**ä**ther; s**e**t; m**ē**; **i**t; k**ī**te; **o**x; r**ō**se; **ô** in b**ou**ght; c**oi**n; b**oo**k; t**oo**; f**o**rm; **ou**t; **u**p; **ū**se; t**û**rn; **ə** sound in **a**bout, chick**e**n, penc**i**l, cann**o**n, circ**u**s; **ch**air; **hw** in **wh**ich; ri**ng**; **sh**op; **th**in; **th**ere; **zh** in trea**s**ure.

sly (slĭ) *adj.* Causing difficulty in a playful way.

sneaking (snēk´ ing) *v.* Moving or acting quietly, secretly.

solo (sō´ lō) *n.* Music that one person sings or plays on an instrument.

spooky (spoo´ kē) *adj.* Scary.

squealed (skwēld) *v.* Past tense of **squeal:** To make a loud cry or sound.

sticks (stiks) *n.* Plural of **stick:** A long, thin, piece of wood.

straw (strô) *n.* Dried stems of plants.

sturdy (stûr´ dē) *adj.* Strong.

suggest (səg jest´) *v.* To give or tell an idea.

supposed to (sə pōzd´ too) *v.* Should do something.

symbol (sim´ bəl) *n.* An idea or object that stands for something else.

tarry (târ´ ē) *v.* To delay or wait; to do something slowly.

teddy bear (ted´ ē bâr) *n.* A stuffed toy bear.

teddy bear

thaw (thô) *n.* The time the weather becomes warmer in winter and things melt.

thinks (thingks) *v.* Believes.

thrill (thril) n. A feeling of adventure.

tin (tin) *n.* A kind of metal sometimes used to make cans.

tin

tough (tuf) *adj.* Brave; able to put up with something hard or difficult.

trembling (trem´ bəl ing) *v.* Shaking.

trouble (trub´ əl) *n.* Problems; difficulty.

trudge (truj) *v.* To walk slowly with heavy steps.

tunnels (tun´ əlz) *n.* Plural of **tunnel:** An underground passageway.

twigs (twigz) *n.* Plural of **twig:** Tiny branch.

typical (tip´ i kəl) *adj.* Usual.

U

underground (un´ dər ground´) *n.* Below Earth's surface.

underneath (un´ dər nēth´) *adv.* Below.

United States (ū nīt´ id stāts) *n.* The country we live in which is made of 50 states.

Pronunciation Key: at; lāte; câre; fäther; set; mē; it; kīte; ox; rōse; ô in bought; coin; book; too; form; out; up; ūse; tûrn; ə sound in about, chicken, pencil, cannon, circus; chair; hw in which; ring; shop; thin; there; zh in treasure.

visit (viz´ it) *v.* To go see someone or something.

visitors (viz´ it ûrz) *n.* Plural of **visitor:** Someone who goes to see someone else.

Washington, D.C. (wô´ shing tən dē sē) *n.* The capital of the United States.

White House (wīt hous) *n.* The place the president of the United States lives.

windows (win´ dōz) *n.* Plural of **window:** An opening in a wall or roof of a house that lets in air and light.

windows

wires (wīrz) *v.* Puts lines in for electricity.

wood (wood) *n.* The hard material that covers the trunk and branches of many plants.

wrappers (rap´ ərz) *n.* Plural of **wrapper:** A piece of paper or other covering around an object.

wrestling (res´ling) *n.* A sport in which two people try to hold each other down with strength.

yard (yärd) *n.* The area of ground around a house, school, or other building.

Reading Resources

Reading Comprehension

Comprehension Strategies will help you understand what you are reading.

Summarizing

As you read, ask yourself the following questions:

1. What is this selection about?

2. What is unclear? What is the meaning of the word or sentence? How can I find out?

3. What are the big ideas the writer is trying to get at?

4. Have I said the same thing more than once in my summary?

5. What can I delete from my summary? What is not important?

6. How can I put what I have just read into my own words?

Clarifying

As you read, ask yourself the following questions:

1. What does not make sense? If it is a word, how can I figure it out? Do I use context clues, word analysis, or apposition, or do I need to ask someone or look it up in the dictionary or glossary?

2. If a sentence is long and complicated, have I reread it as well as the sentences before and after it to see if the meaning is clarified? Have I read the sentence part by part to see exactly what is confusing?

Have I tried to restate the sentence in my own words?

3. The paragraph is long and full of details. What can I do to understand it? I can take notes, I can reread it more slowly, or I can discuss it with someone.

4. What is the main idea of what I just read?

5. Can I put what I just read into my own words?

Asking Questions

As you read, ask yourself the following questions:

1. What do I already know about this topic?

2. What else would I like to know about this topic?

3. What questions do I think the author will answer as I read this selection?

4. How does this information connect to what I already know about the topic?

5. How does this information connect to the unit theme?

6. What is not making sense in this selection?

7. What is interfering with my understanding?

Predicting

As you read, ask yourself the following questions:

1. What clues in the text can help me predict what will happen next?

2. What clues in the text tell me what probably will not happen next?

Confirming Predictions

As you read, ask yourself the following questions:

1. How was my prediction confirmed?

2. Why was my prediction not confirmed?

3. What clues did I miss that would have helped me make a better prediction?

Making Connections

As you read, ask yourself the following questions:

1. What does this remind me of? What else have I read like this?

2. How does this connect with something in my own life?

3. How does this connect with other selections I have read?

4. How does this connect with what is going on in the world today?

5. How does this relate to other events or topics I have studied in social studies or science?

Visualizing

As you read, ask yourself the following questions:

1. What picture do the words create in my mind? What specific words help create feelings, actions, and settings in my mind?

2. What can I see, hear, smell, taste, and/or feel in my mind?

3. How does this picture help me understand what I am reading?

4. How does my mental picture extend beyond the words in the text?

Comprehension Skills will help you understand the purpose and organization of a selection.

Author's Point of View

Author's point of view tells who is telling the story. When a story is told by a character in the story, it is told in first-person point of view. The character uses the pronouns *I, my, me,* and *we.* When a story is told in third-person point of view, the story is told by someone who is not part of the story. The pronouns *he/she, him/her, they,* and *it* are used.

Sequence

Sequence is the order in which things happen in a story. The more you know about the sequence of events in a story, the better you will understand the story. Writers use time and order words such as *first, then, finally, tonight,* and *yesterday* to tell the order of events.

Main Idea and Details

The main idea is what the story or paragraph is mostly about. Writers use details to tell more about or explain the main idea.

Compare and Contrast

To compare means to tell how things, events, or characters are alike. To contrast means to tell how things, events, or characters are different. Writers use compare and contrast to make an idea clearer or to make a story more interesting.

Cause and Effect

Cause-and-effect relationships help you understand connections between the events in a story. The cause is why something happens. The effect is what happens as a result. A cause produces an effect.

Classify and Categorize

An author often includes many details in a story. Putting the like things together, or classifying those like things into categories, helps you see how actions, events, and characters from a story are related.

Author's Purpose

An author writes for different purposes or reasons. An author may write to entertain, to inform, or to persuade. If an author is writing to entertain, he or she may use amusing words or exciting events. If an author is writing to inform, he or she may use facts that can be proven or may explain steps in a process. If an author is writing to persuade, he or she includes his or her opinions about something.

Drawing Conclusions

You draw conclusions when you take information in the selection about a character or an event and use this information to make a statement or conclusion about that character or event.

Making Inferences

You make inferences about characters or events in a story by using information the author provides and adding that to what you already know. Making Inferences helps you better understand the events in a story.

Reality and Fantasy

In a realistic story, people, animals, and objects do things they could do in the real world. However, in a fantasy, people, animals, and objects do things they could not do in the real world.

Vocabulary Strategies

Context Clues

When you come to an unfamiliar word in your reading, look for clues in the sentence or in the sentences around it. These clues might help you understand the meaning of the word.

Apposition

Sometimes the word is defined within the text. In apposition, the word is followed by the definition, which is set off by commas.

Word Analysis

Looking at the parts of a word can help you figure out the word's meaning. For example, the word *unhappy* can be broken down into meaning word parts: the prefix *un-*, which means "not," and the base word *happy*. Knowing the meaning of each part will help you come up with the definition "not happy."

Discussion Strategies

Summarizing

1. I think the main idea is …
2. I think an important supporting detail is…
3. I think the best evidence to support the main idea is …
4. To summarize …
5. I learned …
6. I can conclude …

Clarifying

1. I have a question about …
2. I am still confused about …
3. Does anyone know …
4. Could we clarify …
5. I figured out that …
6. I had difficulty understanding _____ because …

7. I still do not understand …

8. What did the author mean when he or she wrote _____?

9. Who can help me clarify _____?

10. Why did the author _____?

Asking Questions

1. What if …

2. How do we know …

3. I wonder what would happen if …

4. What do we know about …

5. I wonder why the author chose to . . .

Predicting

1. I expect …

2. I predict …

3. Based on _____, I predict …

4. I can support my prediction by/with …

5. I would like to change my prediction because …

6. My prediction was confirmed when/by …

7. My prediction was not confirmed because…

Making Connections

1. This made me think …

2. I was reminded of …

3. This selection reminds me of what we read in _____ because …

4. This selection connects to the unit theme because…

5. I would like to make a connection to …

6. I found _____ interesting because …

7. This author's writing reminds me of …

Visualizing

1. When I read _____, I visualized …

2. The author's words _____ helped me visualize …

3. Visualizing helped me understand …
4. The author made the story really come alive by …

Adjusting Reading Speed

1. I decided to read this more slowly because …
2. I found I needed to slow down when …

Other Discussion Starters

Personal Response

1. I did not know that …
2. I liked the part where …
3. I agree with _____ because …
4. I disagree with _____ because …
5. The reason I think _____ is …
6. I was surprised to find out …

7. I like the way the author developed the character by …

Agreeing with a Response

1. I agree because …
2. I see what you mean because…

Disagreeing with a Response

1. I disagree because …
2. I think we can agree that _____, but …

Grade One English-Language Arts Content Standards

Reading

1.0 Word Analysis, Fluency, and Systematic Vocabulary Development

Students understand the basic features of reading. They select letter patterns and know how to translate them into spoken language by using phonics, syllabication, and word parts. They apply this knowledge to achieve fluent oral and silent reading.

Concepts About Print

1.1 Match oral words to printed words.
1.2 Identify the title and author of a reading selection.
1.3 Identify letters, words, and sentences.

Phonemic Awareness

1.4 Distinguish initial, medial, and final sounds in single-syllable words.
1.5 Distinguish long-and short-vowel sounds in orally stated single-syllable words (e.g., bit/bite).
1.6 Create and state a series of rhyming words, including consonant blends.
1.7 Add, delete, or change target sounds to change words (e.g., change cow to how; pan to an).
1.8 Blend two to four phonemes into recognizable words (e.g., /c/ a/ t/ = cat; /f/ l/ a/ t/ = flat).
1.9 Segment single-syllable words into their components (e.g., /c/ a/ t/ = cat; /s/ p/ l/ a/ t/ = splat; /r/ i/ ch/ = rich).

Decoding and Word Recognition

1.10 Generate the sounds from all the letters and letter patterns, including consonant blends and long-and short-vowel patterns (i.e., phonograms), and blend those sounds into recognizable words.
1.11 Read common, irregular sight words (e.g., the, have, said, come, give, of).
1.12 Use knowledge of vowel digraphs and r- controlled letter-sound associations to read words.
1.13 Read compound words and contractions.
1.14 Read inflectional forms (e.g., -s, -ed, -ing) and root words (e.g., look, looked, looking).
1.15 Read common word families (e.g., -ite, -ate).
1.16 Read aloud with fluency in a manner that sounds like natural speech.

Vocabulary and Concept Development

1.17 Classify grade-appropriate categories of words (e.g., concrete collections of animals, foods, toys).

2.0 Reading Comprehension

Students read and understand grade-level-appropriate material. They draw upon a variety of comprehension strategies as needed (e.g., generating and responding to essential questions, making predictions, comparing information from several sources). The selections in Recommended Literature, Kindergarten Through Grade Twelve illustrate the quality and complexity of the materials to be read by students. In addition to their regular school reading, by grade four, students read one-half million words annually, including a good representation of grade-level-appropriate narrative and expository text (e.g., classic and contemporary literature, magazines, newspapers, online information). In grade one, students begin to make progress toward this goal.

Structural Features of Informational Materials

2.1 Identify text that uses sequence or other logical order.

Comprehension and Analysis of Grade-Level-Appropriate Text

2.2 Respond to who, what, when, where, and how questions.
2.3 Follow one-step written instructions.
2.4 Use context to resolve ambiguities about word and sentence meanings.
2.5 Confirm predictions about what will happen next in a text by identifying key words (i.e., signpost words).
2.6 Relate prior knowledge to textual information.
2.7 Retell the central ideas of simple expository or narrative passages.

3.0 Literary Response and Analysis

Students read and respond to a wide variety of significant works of children's literature. They distinguish between the structural features of the text and the literary terms or elements (e.g., theme, plot, setting, characters). The selections in Recommended Literature, Kindergarten Through Grade Twelve illustrate the quality and complexity of the materials to be read by students.

Narrative Analysis of Grade-Level-Appropriate Text

3.1 Identify and describe the elements of plot, setting, and character(s) in a story, as well as the story's beginning, middle, and ending.
3.2 Describe the roles of authors and illustrators and their contributions to print materials.
3.3 Recollect, talk, and write about books read during the school year.

Writing

1.0 Writing Strategies

Students write clear and coherent sentences and paragraphs that develop a central idea. Their writing shows they consider the audience and purpose. Students progress through the stages of the writing process (e.g., prewriting, drafting, revising, editing successive versions).

Organization and Focus
1.1 Select a focus when writing.
1.2 Use descriptive words when writing.

Penmanship
1.3 Print legibly and space letters, words, and sentences appropriately.

2.0 Writing Applications (Genres and Their Characteristics)

Students write compositions that describe and explain familiar objects, events, and experiences. Student writing demonstrates a command of standard American English and the drafting, research, and organizational strategies outlined in Writing Standard 1.0.

Using the writing strategies of grade one outlined in Writing Standard 1.0, students:

2.1 Write brief narratives (e.g., fictional, autobiographical) describing an experience.
2.2 Write brief expository descriptions of a real object, person, place, or event, using sensory details.

Written and Oral English Language Conventions

The standards for written and oral English language conventions have been placed between those for writing and for listening and speaking because these conventions are essential to both sets of skills.

1.0 Written and Oral English Language Conventions

Students write and speak with a command of standard English conventions appropriate to this grade level.

Sentence Structure
1.1 Write and speak in complete, coherent sentences.

Grammar
1.2 Identify and correctly use singular and plural nouns.
1.3 Identify and correctly use contractions (e.g., isn't, aren't, can't, won't) and singular possessive pronouns (e.g., my/ mine, his/ her, hers, your/s) in writing and speaking.

Punctuation
1.4 Distinguish between declarative, exclamatory, and interrogative sentences.
1.5 Use a period, exclamation point, or question mark at the end of sentences.
1.6 Use knowledge of the basic rules of punctuation and capitalization when writing.

Capitalization
1.7 Capitalize the first word of a sentence, names of people, and the pronoun *I*.

Spelling
1.8 Spell three-and four-letter short-vowel words and grade-level-appropriate sight words correctly.

Listening and Speaking

1.0 Listening and Speaking Strategies

Students listen critically and respond appropriately to oral communication. They speak in a manner that guides the listener to understand important ideas by using proper phrasing, pitch, and modulation.

Comprehension
1.1 Listen attentively.
1.2 Ask questions for clarification and understanding.
1.3 Give, restate, and follow simple two-step directions.

Organization and Delivery of Oral Communication
1.4 Stay on the topic when speaking.
1.5 Use descriptive words when speaking about people, places, things, and events.

2.0 Speaking Applications (Genres and Their Characteristics)

Students deliver brief recitations and oral presentations about familiar experiences or interests that are organized around a coherent thesis statement. Student speaking demonstrates a command of standard American English and the organizational and delivery strategies outlined in Listening and Speaking Standard 1.0.

Using the speaking strategies of grade one outlined in Listening and Speaking Standard 1.0, students:

2.1 Recite poems, rhymes, songs, and stories.
2.2 Retell stories using basic story grammar and relating the sequence of story events by answering who, what, when, where, why, and how questions.
2.3 Relate an important life event or personal experience in a simple sequence.
2.4 Provide descriptions with careful attention to sensory detail.